MANAGING POWER THROUGH LATERAL NETWORKING

Margaret Brindle and Lisa A. Mainiero

Q

QUORUM BOOKS
Westport, Connecticut • London

Library of Congress Cataloging-in-Publication Data

Brindle, Margaret.
    Managing power through lateral networking / Margaret Brindle
and Lisa A. Mainiero.
        p.   cm.
    Includes bibliographical references and index.
    ISBN 1–56720–334–5 (alk. paper)
    1. Organizational effectiveness.   2. Organizational behavior.   3.
Corporate culture.   I. Mainiero, Lisa A.   II. Title.
    HD58.9 .B75   2000
    650.1'3—dc21   99–27822

British Library Cataloguing in Publication Data is available.

Library of Congress Catalog Card Number: 99–27822
ISBN: 1–56720–334–5

First published in 2000

Quorum Books, 88 Post Road West, Westport, CT 06881
An imprint of Greenwood Publishing Group, Inc.
www.quorumbooks.com

Printed in the United States of America

The paper used in this book complies with the
Permanent Paper Standard issued by the National
Information Standards Organization (Z39.48–1984).

10   9   8   7   6   5   4   3   2   1

Contents

Acknowledgments

Writing acknowledgments for a book is never easy. There are many people to thank, and someone is always forgotten. We would like to begin by thanking a great scholar—our mentor who brought us together in this work—Jerry Salancik. He taught us much about power, politics, and dependency relationships and developed one of the first M.B.A. courses in power and politics at Stanford University in the early 1980s.

We thank our M.B.A. students, whose experiences, real-life cases, and dilemmas formed the underpinnings of this book. It is for the talented and ambitious practioners who struggle within the complex set of power and dependencies in lateral relationships that this book is primarily designed.

We also extend our appreciation to our respective universities. The opportunity to teach at Carnegie Mellon University has been a rich laboratory, where many hundreds of M.B.A. students provided their deeply personal struggles and insights about work problems in settings from this country and across the globe. At Fairfield University, Dean Walter Ryba in particular supported this effort by providing a sabbatical for one of the authors to work on this book. In helping to move the book to its final stage, we thank Alan Sturmer, our editor.

We also thank David Mangini who developed the artwork for the book. His talent with computer-aided design, his objective critical views and his unswerving personal support and unconditional love are much appreciated, especially by one of the authors in particular. And we thank

Peter N. Stearns for sound editorial advice and most important for listening to endless ramblings about the nature of lateral relationships. His personal love and support has been an unmeasurable part of moving the work from concept to completion.

On a personal note, we thank our families. We also lovingly thank our children who individually and as a group, suffered for and will eventually benefit from this book: Michael-David and Mariana Mangini, and Luke, Timothy, Stephen, and Patrick Brindle. It is our hope that as they grow and enter the world of work, with all of its complexity and excitement, that the model provided in this work may serve them well in managing their own lateral relationships in an increasingly dynamic business environment. They continue to inspire us with their simple love and trusting devotion. As we watch their worlds change from dolls, Legos, yo-yos, and the puzzles of play to working within and contributing to their chosen fields, we dedicate this book to their journey ahead.

PART I

UNDERSTANDING LATERAL NETWORKS AND POWER

This book was written to fill a gap. "A gap?" you ask incredously. Books on management take up more space in bookstores than should be allowed by law. Indeed, books on management abound, but they fall into two major categories, neither of which is adequate for today's managers. On the one hand, there is a wide array of self-help books that promote management skills. These books tell you that interpersonal skills and the personal mastery of time, attitude, and perseverance will make you a success. On the other end of the spectrum, books promoting theories about how we can fix entire organizations with new, utopian theories surface almost as prolifically. Such theories as "Total Quality Management and Reengineering" fit this bill. Proclaiming new solutions for entire organizations, either business or industry, these books also promise fairly smooth sailing over the realities of organizational complexity.

Yet, in the seemingly endless stream of self-help books and large-scale, organization-wide problem solving, there remains a gap. The gap is reality. The gap is filled with people who have failed. The gap is the land of frustrated managers, unable to get things done.

The fact is that all the amount of self-help in the world—all the charm, interpersonal influence, and time management—is small potatoes in today's politically complex organizational and business worlds. Although there is a place for individual skills and a certain amount of hutzpah, these skills are inadequate in today's business world. In short, one cannot charm, manipulate, influence, cajole, or con one's way through the labyrinth of political workings that make up today's laterally constructed organizations.

Idealized theories of organizations miss the mark as well. For decades, since men (and now women) first decided to work in organizational settings rather than at home, management gurus have expounded upon ideas and ideals for the best way to perform that work. Since the days of Frederick Taylor and his "one best way of doing things," to the Total Quality Management paradigm of the 1980s, no one theory of organizing work has provided a very satisfactory road map through the complexity residing in organizational contexts. To be sure, some theories have helped orient us to a semblance of order, coordination, and organizing, and have also certainly made managers feel like they knew what they were doing (at least most of the time), the fact remains that there are no utopian theories for managing complexity in people-rich settings. The main problem with the individual, self-help approach is that it focuses on the individual and ignores the context; the organization wide theories construct hypothetical views of idealized organizations.

Our starting point for this work is that organizations are far too complex for both individualized, self-help, or idealized management theories to enacapsulate. And they leave behind many frustrated managers with failed ideas and faulty plans sitting on the cutting room floor. How do we know? We know because many hundreds of frustrated, and talented individuals have filtered back to school to obtain higher degrees in management. They come back not just for new titles or the prospect of more money. They come back to learn how to be effective—how to get things done—how not to fail, again. We see them in our M.B.A. classrooms. Others call us on the phone in our consulting business:

"I did everything right, but then I was let go."

"My plan would have saved them a half million the first year, but no, it wasn't the way they do things around there."

"My information system would have given that bank the coordination system it needed to maintain customer accounts. I worked on it for almost a year. Then the union blocked it. I can't believe my boss tossed it. I quit."

"All I wanted was a division transfer. It would have made sense. They trained me and spent money. Now they've lost me because I was out of the box."

So go some of the comments of our disillusioned M.B.A. students. Many of them hit brick walls, not in titles and even promotions, but in their own sense of failed expectations about their capabilities, achievements, and effectiveness. Many of them have moved through the ranks of the career ladder with outward success, but in pure and simple terms, they can't get their good ideas accomplished.

And so, we have been interested in why so many smart people have failed over the past ten years. We have been privy to too much frustration. This frustration is exacerbated by a number of things. First, the good ideas have merit, and the people trying to enact them know it. Their businesses need to change to keep pace, and often the ideas our clients have proposed would be just the thing to help those businesses achieve a higher level of success. Many young workers, professionals, and managers have been educated to expect that they will be successful with their knowledge, superior education, abilities, and training. Not being successful in their organizational problems generates great frustration. The frustration of failed good ideas, we have found, is often quite startling.

Many turn to management books promoting individualized skills— "If only I had the right formula of interpersonal skills, or utopian management theories." Many dream of a better place to work. We laugh at the cartoon, "Dilbert," whose popularity is no accident. New formulas for utopia abound, and we laugh because most of us work where "Dilbert" works. We relate to the "new plan"; centralization versus decentralization and back again, or total quality and employee participation. Today it is strategic planning; tomorrow the plans are scrapped by an unpredicted takeover, or you lose despite the best-laid plans because somebody else won favor with the boss. We think this translates as confusion for managers and workers alike, as they strive to capture the new rules and norms in shifting organizational structures.

By now you know this book is not about a new formula for instant personal or organizational success. This book instead is about the complexities of work relationships in lateral settings, and how interpersonal power relationships must be analyzed before anyone can be effective at work.

We wrote this book because of all the smart people we have worked with who seemed to lack the skills for getting things accomplished. In many cases this was because they lacked knowledge of organizational reality. We studied hundreds of failures in order to determine how to succeed.

So, what is the reality? The reality is that there are building blocks of organizational life. It is the lateral relationships that comprise businesses. It can be distilled to the simple, but sometimes hard to understand, basics of resources and dependencies. We present these building blocks in the first section of this book, not in abstract theory, but rather as elements that can be diagnosed and understood in all organizations. Working from real cases, the first half of this book demonstrates how to understand organizational complexities and the lateral relationships that comprise them. We build a strategic model, applicable to all manner of intractable organizational problems. Then, in the second part of the book, we provide themes that we have taken from the hundreds of failed ideas and innovations from M.B.A. students and clients.

The reality is that organizations are complex places and are getting more so. As we shift management paradigms from hierarchical to vertical structures, from rules and procedures to understandings and concensus, and from formal authority to lateral power, the quintessential skills for success are also changing. Managers don't merely need the abstact "people" skills. They need skills at understanding the context—how the people and their relative power fit together. They need to analyze, diagnose, and plan rigorously within complex lateral relationships.

This book is about understanding organizations and their building blocks. It is about learning how to solve your intractable organizational problems, one by one, with as much rigor, planning, diagnosis, and execution of detailed strategy as you would approach any other, more tangible, more quantitative business problem. It provides tough analysis and tough tools based on real managers and their very real problems.

As one student lamented, "I thought something was wrong with me—that I couldn't get what I needed for my squadron. Everything we learned in our military leadership courses was about positive thinking, endurance and keeping, at all times an, 'I can do it mentality.' So, when you get out there and you're in charge and you can't get supplies, I felt like a personal failure. I kept trying, knocking on the same doors, so to speak. The analysis I've learned here showed me that endurance and personal will, coupled with all the interpersonal leadership traits in the world doesn't give you success, unless you also understand the inner political workings of the organization—even when it's the military."

We submit there are real reasons why so many managers encounter stone walls when attempting to solve business problems that escape standard textbook solutions. Most of these problems concern misunderstandings about the political realities that arise from managing lateral relationships effectively. But good ideas alone are simply not sufficient to make things happen in most organizations. Lateral relationships must be managed, and to be managed, they must be diagnosed, analyzed, and understood.

What makes this book unusual is that we offer diagnostic tools, a carefully tested theory, and carefully tested strategies. We offer a road map to readers to solve "unsolvable" problems based on the real-life, complex dilemmas of new as well as seasoned managers. We can show readers what buttons to push and which levers to weigh, and when and how to do both. Our book is the result of decades of case material from managers, many of whom have used our methods to take their good ideas and turn them into workable realities.

1

Why Good Ideas Fail

Have you ever proposed a good idea to your boss, which he initially rejected, but then watched it being implemented later, while you miss getting the credit? Or have you had a wonderful idea to change work processes that for one reason or another failed miserably from the moment you presented your concept? Have you scratched your head, wondering why? If so, this book is for you.

Why do good ideas in firms get passed over so easily? That is the wrong question. A better question to ask is, "Why do smart people with good ideas have such a problem getting things done?" This book is about smart people resolving dilemmas getting things done in their organizations. No doubt you are smart. Of course you have already attended every training program offered by your firm. You probably already have your M.B.A. under your belt or are working on it. You are talented, intelligent, and highly skilled, yet your latest smart idea fell like a lead balloon at your last presentation.

Great ideas fail not because the ideas are academic or trivial. Nor are the people who construct them stupid, lazy, or insipid. Generally, great ideas are constructed by highly intelligent, trained people who know what they are doing. Their ideas result from months of analysis, planning, ingenuity, and creative smarts. These are not fly-by-night ideas. But, nonetheless, they fail.

We have been solving the "unsolveable" problems of managers and technical experts cumulatively for about thirty-five years. We are consultants and M.B.A. educators, and thus write this book with both a pragmatic outlook as well as a theoretical basis. The research data from which we draw our case studies are based on the experiences of more than six-hundred M.B.A. students at Stanford, Carnegie Mellon, and Fairfield University. We also include material from executives, average managers, and clients to round out our sample.

Our book highlights several intriguing case themes that repeat over and over within organizations, as people try to get things done. Although the scenarios vary in detail and the contexts change from consulting firms to manufacturing plants, we find that these running themes allow us to distill patterns. These themes can be categorized into archetypes of the misuse of power and reasons for failure. Most important, as patterns repeat, certain actions can be studied as ones that promote effectiveness in managing repetitive organizational dilemmas.

THE CASE OF PETER

Consider this surprising scenario. A young student, Peter, graduates from a top-tier computer-science program at a well-known university, armed with the latest skills and knowledge. Added to this package is a generally pleasing personality, excellent communication skills, and managerial talent. He lands an enviable position at a reputable information technology firm.

Peter's first assignment was to design a basic information system for a small company client. In relatively short order, Peter designed a system that pulled together some of the latest technology, in a manner he believed was tailor-made for this client. He went beyond the basics of the assignment, and in his zeal to do well, provided an implementation plan that was under budget as well.

As Peter prepared to present his plan, he was approached by one of the client's managers, who said, "Well, we hope your plan isn't like the last one they gave us. I don't know who they thought they were fooling." Peter's presentation went well, but afterward he was surprised when there were no questions. He responded by priding himself on his clarity and polish. He returned to his downtown office with his manager, who was unusually quiet. Finally, his manager said disdainfully, "Well, I was right about you. You kids from Tech U. really think you're smart. Why didn't you tell me you had the implementation plan all spelled out, and for heaven's sake, why did you kill the budget?"

Later that afternoon, the phone rang. It was the general partner of the firm requesting Peter's presence upstairs immediately. The company had called and canceled the contract. Peter received a warning that if he didn't shape up and learn to play with the team, he would be fired within thirty days.

Peter, back in his office, put his head in his hands, wondering what went wrong. The system he had designed was everything the client needed to become a more credible player. It saved them money, coordinated work, and was intelligently below his manager's budget. It was the capstone of his systems training, and he had presented it beautifully and articulately and used his financial skills to keep it under budget. Indeed, if this had been an academic test, Peter would have gotten an "A."

Peter had done a good job, but unfortunately, it was the wrong reality. In this case, Peter was speaking a different language without knowledge of the social context. There had been considerable tension with the client regarding a past system they had intended to implement, and on which they felt they had been "low-balled," meaning that a realistic budget had not been represented. Added to this was the fact that the client did not want a new system that would replace management staff and had specified such. But Peter was unaware of this context, and therefore, made a huge blunder.

Why do talented people have such a difficult time pulling off their organized and efficient ideas? More often than not, we have discovered that the block has to do with routines, structure, issues of turf, affects on systems unseen, and overall, misunderstanding the critical issues of power and politics.

THE CASE OF FRANCINE AND THE SHIPPING CLERKS

Francine, a young, ambitious, and newly minted M.B.A., was excited to have been hired by one of the country's largest mail-order firms. On her first day, she was told by her boss that her success at the firm would depend upon her abilities to troubleshoot and solve innovative problems. After a few months observing how the work of the firm got done, Francine became interested in how the distribution of product lines took place. She noted that the process by which the warehouse personnel filled the trucks that delivered the products seemed inefficient.

Her investigation turned up the following information: The warehouse received orders daily over very sophisticated telecommunications equipment that were then filled in an old-fashioned way by shipping clerks. Each clerk prepared orders for shipping truckloads of products. Each clerk had "ownership" over a particular product line and filled trucks accordingly. But the problem was that the trucks were never full. Orders between six and twenty thousand pounds could have either been sent by common carrier or combined into a cheaper company truck for unloading at multiple stops. At the moment, truckloads were often combined but only within a product line. The decision to combine orders or not was left to the shipping clerks, who were evaluated according to their speed in filling orders. Francine calculated that the firm would save three quarters of a million a year if partial truckloads were combined, regardless of product line.

Francine developed a plan for combining orders, got her boss's approval, and presented the new plan to the shipping clerks. After a week's time it became clear that none of the clerks were using the new system. It turned out that the clerks were quite competitive about their jobs. All the shipping clerks fought against one another to get their orders packed and loaded first. They all sought to identify the fastest and cheapest routes for their product lines. After all, their performance evaluations depended upon the speed with which they filled their orders. The new plan was time-consuming and required that the clerks converse about whose truck was empty and whose was full. The clerks simply did not see themselves as having the time or the inclination for such genteel discussions while they were madly vying for truckload space.

Francine did everything she could think of to get the clerks to cooperate. She reasoned with the clerks that she had identified a better system, and while they agreed, they still didn't change their ways. She presented figures as proof. They agreed to try again. More weeks passed without results. She took the best clerks out for coffee and insisted they cooperate. They smiled politely and said they would. She rolled up her sleeves, went down to the shipping floor, and showed them how to arrange combinations of orders destined for the same region. They said they'd try.

After months of working on this problem, Francine threw in the towel. It was another good idea down the tubes.

WHY GOOD IDEAS OFTEN FAIL

In many business organizations, good ideas often are initiated with great promise only to inexplicably fall by the wayside. New M.B.A.s like Francine complain that the textbooks they so assiduously studied in graduate school simply do not match with the realities of the business world. This leads to great anguish and concern on the part of the M.B.A.s about whether getting the degree was worth it in the first place.

We submit there are reasons—good reasons—why average managers encounter stone walls to business problems that escape standard textbook solutions. We believe most of these problems are caused by misunderstandings about the political realities that arise from managing lateral relationships effectively. Good ideas alone are not sufficient to make things happen in most organizations. Lateral relationships must be managed subtly, effectively, and delicately in order to garner adequate support to get anything done.

This book highlights common mistakes people like Francine make in managing lateral relationships as they go about their business. We believe most of the problems in managing lateral relationships, especially in today's virtual offices, concern misunderstandings about the political realities that arise from the underlying power distributions inherent in organizations. Our book is aimed at the educated and smart manager or technical expert who knows what to do, but generally has a difficult time putting the right idea into action.

POLITICAL NAIVETÉ AS A BUSINESS PROBLEM

The major failing of otherwise good managers is one of political naiveté. Francine, as a young M.B.A., was trained to think of work as a technical problem, not a social one. Without an understanding of power and how it operates, it is easy to confuse the appearance from the substance of complicated business dilemmas. Vexing organizational problems require creative solutions. Such solutions arise naturally from an understanding of issues of power and politics among lateral relationships within your firm.

This was Francine's problem, which became clear once she hired a consultant to find out what went wrong. The consultant found that Francine had been operating under false assumptions. She had the impression that the shipping clerks need only change their job habits to cooperate in distributing the firm's major product line. Therefore, Francine had erroneously concluded that her failure was due to the clerks not getting along and being too competitive. But upon observing the situation, this assessment was not entirely accurate. Clerks were friendly to one another during breaks and at lunch. Friendship had little to do with the situation. On the job, the clerks were competitive largely because they were competing for the same scarce resources— trucks, packers, loaders, and warehouse priorities. The demands for distribution for each product line differed. Orders bumped against one another, and clerks served as brokers of merchandise. They traded promises between truckers, carriers, and salespeople. In the words of one veteran, "You succeed at this job by building relationships. This allows you to draw upon those relationships for favors. You do favors for others also. Sometimes a carrier needs to fill a truck destined for south Florida. So you send a partial load that way rather than wait to combine it with another order in a few days. Later, when you need a favor for a rush order, you're not afraid to ask for a kind gesture in return. So it all works out somehow."

In this case, Francine had a good idea. Her idea should have worked, and it might have worked had she approached the situation differently. But new managers like Francine often think that because they're brilliant (which they are), because they have bright ideas (which they do), and because they have the good intentions of the organization in their minds and in their souls and in their hearts, that this is in and of itself sufficient to be able to do good things in your firm. The problem is that it is not sufficient.

Francine's was a classic fundamental error of ignorance of the importance of the social organization and context and its relationship to power and influence. Power in organizations, especially in lateral relationships, follows the social lines of work. Managers who ignore this find that their good ideas are quickly set aside.

THE ENGINEERING SELECTION CASE

This is the case of two brilliant engineers, Don and Ron, in a highly respected manufacturing firm. Both of the engineers were young, dedicated, thoughtful, and knowledgeable about their jobs. They had excellent reputations as production engineers and were well thought of by all who encountered their work.

The problem Don and Ron faced was that their firm needed to install a new manufacturing control system—a system that would have a major and long-term effect on managing the production work of the firm. In other words, this new system would dramatically alter the way in which work on the production line would be accomplished.

This highly respected firm had an MIS department whose responsibility it was to select and purchase the computer equipment to be used by the firm. But Don and Ron also were computer jocks, and they were the ones who would be directly affected by the product choice. And of course, as these things go, they had some ideas of their own. They sharply disagreed with the MIS department's recommendations about what was the best equipment.

What erupted in this case was a classic conflict between line and staff responsibilities. The typical division of labor that exists in most large conglomerates consists of groups that develop expertise on a particular subject and other groups who implement and produce the goods and services offered by the firm. The implementation groups, or the line organization, are supposed to take advantage of the advice of the staff organization because they are too busy producing goods and services to do the research on their own. It is thought to be both inefficient and ineffective to do otherwise. The trouble is that this division of labor sets forth potential for conflict in situations similar to this.

Because Don and Ron were trained to think in terms of logic and reason, they decided that the best alternative was to go to their boss, who was the head of production. They asked if they might evaluate alternative equipment, since they would be the ones who would be saddled with it eventually. Their boss consulted with the boss of the MIS department, and after some sensitive discussion, the two agreed to let the engineers check it out. Don and Ron spent a lot of valuable work time with experts from a nearby university known for its computing and computer knowledge. The computer experts sided with the engineers and provided the facts and figures Don and Ron needed to buttress their case. Don and Ron returned to their boss, armed with the facts, figures, and advice from the official computer experts, certain that they had the answer to this rational and logical problem secured.

The problem resulting from this case is that the two brilliant engineers analyzed this problem in terms of its merits rather than what it was really all about. They thought they were dealing with a basic selection problem. What they did not realize was that they were dealing with a much larger issue—issues about power distribution in the firm.

On the one hand, the MIS department has the authority to make such decisions, and the firm has good reasons to set up a decision-making structure that avoids the problems that may be presented in exactly this type of situation. On the other hand, the manufacturing department should be the ones who have authority to decide on what it takes to manufacture something. They are the production experts, and the firm has good reasons for allowing them domain in their area. How does such a situation get resolved?

The facts and figures the engineers received from the university were met with little interest from the MIS department. After several meetings and long discussions, all the facts and figures did for them was escalate the conflict and reduce their control. This was because the facts and figures had little to do with the important issues that could decide the case: power, managerial discretion, departmental autonomy, and the role of the subunits in the overall activities of the firm.

A DEFINITION: WHAT IS POWER?

Power is potency, or the ability to bring something about, in order to get things done. This definition will serve us well, for it suggests that power is related to the abilities that people or organizations have. This is quite true, in that power is partly brought about by human capabilities and the role those capabilities play in social relationships. Power is also derived from the structure of the social situation. Organizationally, power translates into action. Power is the capacity or capability to make things happen.

To begin a serious study of power, it is important to recognize that power rises and falls and is mirrored by a complex set of social relationships. Because organizations are social systems, it is important to remember that the fabric of relationships in which one is embedded are lateral as well as hierarchical. It is a relatively simple matter to deduce who is in power on an organizational chart. But what is often deceiving is that there are power distributions among lateral relationships that are far more complex—and far more important to understand—than those relationships that are pictured on organizational charts.

We tend to assume that those in authority have power, but this is not always the case. The confusion of who has the authority arises because there is a reciprocal relationship between the two concepts of power and authority. Power serves to distribute authority and is itself a source of power. It is this property—the hierarchical nature of the concept—that most distinguishes power from authority. Power is not the same as influence. We can be influential without power and powerful without influence. If the two were the same, we could not get anything accomplished through others, since we often lack power. The fact that we need others to accomplish something is an indication that we lack power.

MYTHS ABOUT POWER

Power is one of the last "dirty" words in organizational parlance. Quite possibly, we may be more comfortable talking about gender, diversity, and yes, even sex and sexual discrimination than power. This is largely because to talk about power means we admit to thinking about power and that brings into question our moralistic posture. If we want to "have more power," we are viewed as crass and transparent—to be "political" somehow demeans credibility. So, we safely disregard talking about power.

The assumptions here are dangerous. We assume that being political equates to being sleazy, conjuring up images of windbags without original ideas who resort to palm greasing over effective accomplishments. "Ah, he is political," we say disdainfully of those who manipulate and boast their way into position. And sometimes this image is justified, as we all know people who seem to maneuver into positions while lacking substance.

But the opposite is equally problematic. Because power and politics have such a negative connotation, we avoid talking about it. Worse, we avoid learning about it and then shake our heads when we are unable to accomplish our objectives. Let's look at some common myths about power that prevent people from using power appropriately and being effective.

Myth 1: I Don't Do Power; I Just Try to Mind My Own Business

We all know individuals who seem to spend much of their work lives complaining about the problems and ineffectiveness of the organizations in which they work and the "awful" leaders who manage them. There are people who always complain about the day-shift people, the night-shift people, the idiots on the other team, the morons in the other department, or the slackers whose tasks precede mine. It's always them and not us. We are affected by the power structures of our work places, whether we choose to acknowledge power or not. And quite frequently, people who ignore power or fail to recognize it become relatively powerless. Sometimes, the frustration generated by powerlessness causes people to be more corrupted by its influence than they might be otherwise.

Along with our general disdain for acknowledging power is the resultant tendency to misattribute problems in organizations. "We versus them" mentalities besiege and overtake many people, diminishing overall effectiveness. As long as problems are misattributed, they can't be solved effectively. When the cause of a problem that really has to do with internal culture, power structures, and political workings is attributed to people or externalities, one of two outcomes results. The first is blame. Generally acknowledged as ineffective, blame attributes the problem to the person or group that fails to address or fix the problem. More disdainfully, firing people, which is sometimes a necessity, usually does not address the underlying problem or issues, especially when we have misattributed the cause of the problem in the first place.

More important, applying "fixes," or problem solving as we herald it in M.B.A. curricula, often scores points as activity that is measurable by constituents. But fixes that attack structures and processes are more difficult because of the power distributions that underlie those structures and processes. In balance, restructuring is sometimes effective, as people and processes and customers are brought into closer dialogue. But restructuring, without full consideration of how political issues will be shaped, is weak at best.

Myth 2: Power and Politics Are Only Something to Think about When You're Negotiating Something

There is some tendency for managers to think about power and politics in the context of preparing for negotiation or when they are in a dilemma. "Whose support do I need for this objective?" and "What cleverness can I apply to obtain it?" become the questions posed by smart managers. But we maintain that it is too late to think about power and politics at the negotiating table. The reality is that organizations are political and that's why your last great idea failed miserably. Politics and power are not nasty appendages to organizational life—they are integral to organizational life and your own capability to function and to be effective. In fact, in a substantial way, we are talking about the basic building blocks of organization, from which the more tangible environment, structures, rules, policies, order, decision making, and culture are derived.

Myth 3: Do a Good Job and You Won't Be Bothered by Organizational Politics

Many an accomplished college graduate hits the ground running with a noble attitude. Unfortunately, sometimes they don't get up from that ground when reality hits them square in the face. Many a new manager, and even a newly minted CEO, attack new positions with similar gusto and bravado, determined to do a good job. Few power failures are the result of laziness. Most people who ascribe to managerial positions have no lack of motivation, ambition, or intelligence.

But success in organizations is never based on individual efforts. We like to think that decisions are based on merit, and that a "good job" involves learning and meeting criteria. Our general sense of what constitutes a "good job" is enveloped in a notion of fairness and individual merit. We expect those criteria will be applied fairly in our work places, but rarely is that the case. This is because power and politics cast a long shadow over most organizational decisions. And fairness from a manager's perspective has more to do with what is "fair" from an overall organizational perspective than from an individual's.

WHAT THIS BOOK WILL REVEAL

This book will provide you with the tools you need to analyze and to solve vexing organizational problems. The actions that promote effectiveness surround the central concept of the inverse relationship between power and dependence, as illustrated by our model. In lateral relationships, you depend on others to get done those things you want done. Power and dependence share an inverse relationship, as we shall see in the following chapters and case analyses in this book.

Once you understand the fundamental relationship between dependence and power, you are well on your way to mapping out the situations you face. You will then be able to understand how power arises in a social situation. You also will be able to grasp the unbelievable potential that we all have for being potent, and for getting done what we wish to get done. We will present a model of power that we believe will serve you well in facing most organizational problems. You will find that the resolution to many of these problems starts first with an outward analysis of the situation and the factors that externally control the situation. Based on this analysis you will discover a strategy that will help you resolve your problem in some cases. In other cases, you may choose to walk away. But in either case, the choices you make will be yours to recognize, accept, and potentially control.

2

Who Has Clout and Why in the New Lateral Organization

One of the authors of this book learned about power among lateral relationships firsthand when she was involved in a major consulting project for a large pharmaceutical firm. This firm was organized along product lines so that there was a consumer products division, an agricultural chemicals division, an industrial chemical division, a medical products division, and, of course, a headquarters equipped with enough staff and top brass to run the conglomerate. The consultant was hired by a middle-level personnel manager to develop and administer a series of career consultation workshops for employees in the industrial-chemical division. The workshops were a big hit among the rank and file—primarily chemical engineers and scientists, who were feeling disgruntled with the lack of career opportunities at the firm.

Due to their success, the workshops were then conducted in the consumer-products division, and the material presented was met with the same praise and accolades from the rank-and-file employees. Much discussion ensued as to how to improve career opportunities at the firm. It seemed logical and reasonable to expect that job opportunities could be posted among all the different divisions so that employees could move more easily between divisions. Before this time, if you were hired in one division, you made your career in that division. Transfers across divisions were not allowed.

On the surface, the job tasks performed by the employees were largely similar across divisions, and with certain chemical specialties aside, it was quite possible for movement of personnel across divisions to occur. Thousands of employees worked for this major conglomerate, and ordinarily this would have made the posting of available job openings quite a necessary and useful thing. However, everyone expected that top brass would have a problem with this open-job posting concept, even though the reasons against it were unclear.

The consultant took it upon herself to hold a meeting with the top brass in the executive dining room, ostensibly to discuss the possibilities of enacting this idea and ferret out the causes of resistance. The meeting instead became a witch hunt about "what the people in those divisions are saying about us top brass." Discussion about the job-posting concept took up a mere two minutes worth of meeting time, as the VP for the medical division categorically stated he would not allow it. The career workshops folded soon thereafter because there was no support for open job postings across divisions among the higher levels of management.

While the surface of this case simply appears to be a failed intervention, the subtext of the case tells a different story. It turns out that the firm was starting to fall on hard times and was intent on downsizing its work force. There were limited opportunities for advancement or even lateral transfers because the firm's products were no longer as competitive as they had been in the past. This was true both in the consumer-products division and in the industrial-chemical division, the two divisions where the career workshops had enjoyed such success. But the medical division was riding high on a string of product innovations, and the environment was favorable for medical break-throughs; also, biotech stocks were quite strong at the time.

For these reasons, the medical division was definitely the place to be. They had the most discretionary monies available in their budgets. They were hiring people from the outside on a continual basis. They had numerous innovative projects that were crying out for additional staff. Happy people worked there. The industrial-chemical division was a different story. Its markets were drying up as competition increased. There were concerns about environmental fallout for some of the chemical products produced by the industrial-chemical division. Some of the plants were barely passing their safety inspections. Unhappy people worked there. The industrial division was also a big headache for the top brass. The consumer-products division was also a concern, as the firm's products did not match those of their competition. Numerous questions has arisen in board meetings as to whether to close the consumer-products division, sell it, or incorporate it elsewhere. The agricultural division was doing alright, so there was no reason to do anything other than maintain the status quo in that area.

There was limited reason to encourage job posting across divisions. Everyone wanted to transfer to the medical division, but the medical division wanted no part of rescuing laid-off, lackluster employees with bad attitudes. The medical division enjoyed its place in the firm's pecking order and wanted to maintain the status quo. So why did the top brass allow the career workshops to take place in the two failing divisions in the first place? They wanted their employees in their failing divisions to start thinking about career opportunities elsewhere. Transferring them within the firm was furthest from their minds.

Why did this good idea fail? It failed largely because the consultant was unaware of how power was distributed in that organization. The distribution of power can serve as a reflection of the organization's adaptation to its environment.

THE EXTERNAL CONTROL OF ORGANIZATIONS

We will begin with the premise, developed from the early work of Salancik and Pfeffer (1977), that organizations are externally controlled and therefore must adapt to their environments to survive. To explain what we mean, we must first understand what an organization is.

Every organization, be it a business firm, a community organization, or an educational institution, has certain common characteristics. First, an organization is not the building that displays the sign which tells people its name. Organizations are not hardware. They are software. Organizations consist of groups of people who work together in a system to produce a product or offer a service. The organization itself is the system, but is also everything that relates to that system.

Every organization or system of relationships exists in an industry in which its performance is measured according to the relative performance of other firms in the same industry. This means that its survival is always in question. The firm has a context that is externally controlled. Other firms may produce better goods or services. Other firms may be able to offer products at a more competitive price.

Organizations survive by the extent to which they are effective in managing the elements of their external environment. Their effectiveness is largely derived from the management of demands, particularly the demands of interest groups upon which the organizations depend for resources and support. One interest group of the firm might be its investors. Another might be its customers. Still another might be its suppliers. And of course there are the employees and managers. There are a multitude of other interests as well, such as government regulatory groups, community-service organizations, and groups that monitor changes in the technology and economic climate. These lateral relations groupings—customers, owners, employees suppliers, creditors, competitors, public-interest groups, and government regulatory agencies—constitute that organization's environment. In simpler terms, they comprise the world in which that firm lives.

To survive, organizations require resources. Typically, acquiring resources means the firm must interact with others who control those resources. This means that relationships must be established with the coalitions of interests that the firm faces in its environment. Lateral relationships are established with particular suppliers, customers, and representatives of government agencies. It's through these relationships that goods and services are produced. When you look at organizations in this way, you can begin to see that when reduced to the bare necessities, running an organization is very simple. Basically, it involves managing these lateral relationships effectively so that the firm can survive.

The trick is that all of these lateral relationships are quite complicated because these groups hold independent interests with your firm. For example, your customers want to purchase your product or service below market price. So, to keep your customers happy, you must price your goods or services at cost. But your suppliers can only be kept happy if you pay them enough. Paying them enough may require that you increase the price of your product or service. It also may require that you hold down any salary increases for your employees. Both of the latter groups are bound to be unhappy with such decisions. So the process of managing an organization requires that you balance the interests of one group with another, identifying the point on the tightrope where you can keep the most people happy without alienating others.

UNRAVELING THE MYSTERIES
OF POWER DISTRIBUTION

This becomes interesting when all these relationships are not equal. Some relationships are more central to the survival and success of the organization. Others can legitimately go by the wayside. This is because the power distribution of the organization is derived from the critical contingencies the firm faces in its organizational environment. Power is allocated to lateral subunits within the firm according to each subunit's unique capabilities for dealing with these problems. This follows from strategic-contingencies theory (Salancik and Pfeffer, 1977), which states that those subunits most able to cope with the organization's critical problems and uncertainties acquire power.

In its simplest form, the strategic-contingency theory states that the power accrued by the organizational subunits is based upon the degree to which the firm as a whole is dependent upon for its survival. Typically these are the subunits that are considered to be critical, that hold scarce talent the firm does not have elsewhere, and that can help the firm cope with its uncertainties. For example, strategic-contingency theory implies that when an organization faces a lawsuit that may threaten its existence, the legal department will gain power and influence over organizational decisions. Other groups within the organization recognize the importance of the work that is being done by the legal department and confer higher status upon it. When members of the legal department request additional staff to handle their workload, no one questions their reasoning. When the legal department insists that its budget must be increased tenfold, its request is met with a promise and a smile.

This influence extends beyond handling legal matters to decisions about such areas as product design, advertising, and production. In time, the legal department's budget is increased further. A legion of assistants are hired to handle the work of the senior managers, who then have the luxury of spending their time at their country clubs. But this measure of influence and acquired power lasts only as long as the legal department's skill is needed to solve this key organizational problem. Once the problem is solved, the legal department's expertise is no longer needed in quite the same way. At such a time, the legal department may find its resources to be cut, programs slashed, and a return to the previous, less bountiful existence. This occurs when the critical external problems facing the organization change and another department can provide the solution—for example, the marketing group ascends to power when the competition begins to market its products or services in a way that is attracting your customers.

This creates an interesting paradox: Since those subunits that are in power will use their power to influence organizational decisions in their own favor, a contradiction exists—one that is at the heart of most organizations. Because those in power will not give up their positions easily, they will pursue policies that guarantee their continued domination in the pecking order of the firm. In short, change and stability operate through the same mechanism, and, as a result, the firm will never be completely in phase with its environment or its needs. This is what makes the management of organizations so difficult. While these forces allow firms to become more aligned, they also simultaneously become more misaligned with their environments, creating a constant management conundrum.

To the extent that power is determined by the critical uncertainties and problems facing the organization, and the internal decisions made in the firm reflect such choices, the firm will be aligned with the realities it faces. In short, power facilitates the organization's adaptation to its environment. But because the temptation to remain in power once in power is so strong, it is also quite easy for organizations to become misaligned with their environments. The departments that are in power will define the purposes and goals of the organization in a way that suits their own interests. Those individual interests may not match the reality the firm faces, and they may downplay the anger of the public outcry. Such misalignments lead to organizational failure.

THE YALE MPPM–ADMINISTRATIVE
SCIENCES DEBACLE

To illustrate these points, we offer another case—a case of a respected educational institution that allowed those in power to make decisions which resulted in it becoming misaligned with its environment. In the early 1960s, Yale University created the first doctoral-level program that examined the application of behavioral sciences to management practice. Founded on an interdisciplinary model, the Yale doctoral program incorporated elements of sociology, psychology, political science, economics, anthropology, and other disciplines in the study of management practices. The program was the largest in the nation and gave birth to a number of superb scholars who later shaped the very premises upon which the field is founded.

But by the late 1970s, it was clear that a doctoral program was still not sufficient to compete in Yale's educational environment. Yale and Harvard for years had been archenemies, and it really stuck in the craw of the esteemed members of the Yale Corporation Board that Harvard M.B.A.s were all the rage. So, the Yale MPPM program was developed.

The MPPM program was created to train students who would compete on the same level as the Harvard M.B.A., but with a public-sector emphasis. Because there was considerable talent among the administrative-science doctoral faculty, the task of developing the curriculum for the new MPPM program fell upon them. Of course, the administrative-science faculty designed the new program with a considerable infusion of behavioral-science principles. The flagship first-year course for the new students was a "touchy–feely" group dynamics course in which students were taught how to improve their interpersonal and group relationships. It was taught partly as a team-building retreat-type experience so that students would bond together from the start. The program emphasized the principles of cooperation—not competition—of power sharing, not aggrandizement.

But the MPPM students were evaluated by recruiters in the same competitive marketplace as Harvard's and other schools' M.B.A.s. Over time, it became known in the business world that with regard to the Yale MPPMs, while they were nice people, they lacked the "killer instinct" that Harvard bred into its graduates. This caused Yale students to be viewed as less attractive for premier job positions (an interesting comment on the state of the marketplace). Another difficulty was that the program attracted those from the public sector who wanted to make the crossover to the private sector; not the other way around, which the initial program had originally intended. MPPM students also were accused of knowing far too much about behavioral science and not enought about marketing techniques and financial-statement analysis.

This feedback did not sit well with the members of the Yale Corporation Board, who wanted the program to be as strong as other Ivy League M.B.A. programs, Harvard included. Resources were poured into the school so that star financial and marketing faculty could be hired. Immediately upon their arrival, they became incensed at the overwhelming behavioral science emphasis within the MPPM curriculum. When were students to take their upper-level financial courses? A contest of wills developed between the original, highly respected behavioral-science faculty, who had doctoral students at their disposal, and the new MPPM finance and marketing faculty, who had no doctoral program. The faculty clashes became legendary. Intriguing tales were told of faculty members refusing to speak to one another; tempers flaring and fists pounding on tables at faculty meetings; and various acts of academic backstabbing. Deans came and went—none had any luck controlling faculty prima donnas.

So the members of the Yale Corporation, who were annoyed at the whole thing, hired a new dean—a nonacademic, financial business-type who indeed did have the killer instinct that so many of the MPPM students supposedly lacked. He demonstrated his killer instinct almost immediately with two swift actions: He fired the junior behavioral-science faculty, and he discontinued the administrative-science doctoral program.

So what happened here? Were the new dean's actions necessary? While the sympathies of the academic world lay on the side of the fired junior faculty, and all mourned the loss of the premier doctoral program, an analysis of the power distributions within an organization yields a different conclusion. In situations like these, organizations fail to adapt to their environments. As a consequence of these external pressures, organizational crises develop. Organizations with entrenched power structures find it difficult to change and adapt in response to new organizational problems.

It could be argued that Yale's behavioral-science faculty had become too entrenched in their power, causing a lack of adaptation to the M.B.A. environment. A number of clear messages from the outside suggested that there was a need to produce a more well-rounded student. But the faculty members who represented the dominant coalition failed to respond to these data. Instead, they continued to pursue their own agendas in a Pollyannaish sort of way, defining goals and purposes of the organization in ways that best suited their own interests. "Why should we train our students along traditional lines?" they would respond when questioned about their methods. "We are producing a unique commodity—a student who will be able to manage effectively because of his or her behavioral-science training. Therefore it is right and good that we pursue our own agendas." This illustrates precisely what happens when the dominant coalition oversteps its boundaries and neglects the prospect of a changing environment. Organizations that fail to adapt crash.

It is interesting to note that often crises, such as the one depicted in this case, serve to reorganize the power structure of the organization. At Yale, all but two of the behavioral-science faculty remained. The financial faculty, therefore, took over the curriculum and redesigned it with a minimum of behavioral-science material.

Power among lateral relationships emerges under conditions of conflict, and this conflict typically is generated because one party is not getting enough of something that he or she needs. The power to define what is critical in an organization is no small feat. This is why administration can be considered one of the most precarious of occupations; it is management's job to make certain at all times that the internal power distribution of the firm is accurately aligned with the critical contingencies the firm faces in its external environment. What is so necessary for top management to understand is that the critical contingencies facing the organization at any time may change. When they do, it is reasonable to expect that the power of individuals and subgroups within the firm will also be altered.

THE PHARMACEUTICAL COMPANY CASE REVISITED

Now that a basic understanding of the mechanisms that underlie the distribution of power in the firm are in place, we can reexamine the previous case of the pharmaceutical company in a different light.

We stated that the reason that this perfectly reasonable and logical idea for open-job posting failed was because the consultant was unaware how power was distributed in that organization. At the time, the industrial and consumer products divisions had fallen on hard times. This was not true for the medical and agricultural divisions, which were going like gangbusters. In the past, the industrial-chemical division had been the mainstay of the firm's business operations. The business was originally founded as an industrial-chemical manufacturer and in time had expanded to include pharmaceutical and chemicals for other areas, thus the development of the medical, agricultural, and even the consumer-products divisions.

Power is distributed within organizations according to each subunit's unique capabilities for solving the problems presented by the external environment. In the case of this firm, its problems were defined by poor financial performance. The medical division was the only division that was producing a profit, so it was accorded respect. Its profits were solving a key organizational problem. The other divisions were problematic in a variety of ways—environmental manufacturing concerns that caused a public outcry, disgruntled employee hassles, and draining company resources. Obviously, for the reasons described, the medical division held power. It was even widely rumored that the medical division president would become the chief operating officer of the entire conglomerate.

One result of the power that a lateral subunit holds is that it can be a source of influence in obtaining benefits for the employees of that subunit. In this case, the medical division had the best location in the company. It had the best company cafeteria with the best food. It had the most exciting projects going on. Within the division, there were numerous career opportunities and abundant resources. Part of the reason why everyone wanted to move to the medical division was that because resources were so abundant, scientists were allowed the luxury of investigating their own ideas on company time for a few hours each week. This level of autonomy was unheard of at other company locations.

Because power affects the definition of what goals the organization should be pursuing and affects the criteria by which decisions are made, there is a feedback loop, such that the current power distribution of an organization among lateral subunits affects the definition of needs, which in turn also affects how decisions are made. There was no return for the medical division in allowing open-job posting. They instead saw a host of problems. Why should they open their doors to disgruntled refugees from the other divisions? They themselves had never had it so good. Consequently, they refused to allow it. Because the head of the medical division was in power, his decision went unquestioned.

Because power is a source of influence for the subunits and individual employees in organizations, it influences the critical decisions that are made. The critical decisions that can be influenced include but are not limited to staffing the organization, setting budgets, creating and maintaining reporting relationships, and the determination of what the important goals and strategies of the firm should be. Clearly career planning was not a priority of the medical division, in spite of the clearly articulated needs in the other lateral divisions.

Ultimately, the top brass made a series of decisions to reduce the work force but keep both the consumer-products and industrial-chemical divisions after all. Good employees ended up leaving the firm, disgruntled and angry at the uncertainty of it all. Marginal employees remained in both divisions. Two years later, the consultant was approached again to return and do more career workshops, but a different kind. The reason was that the firm now had the need to retain employees because employee turnover had reached crisis proportions.

A similar epilogue occurred in the Yale MPPM case. Years later, bad publicity had affected the school's ability to recruit top quality students. A team of outside faculty were called in to assess the curriculum so that it could be made more attractive. Their conclusion was that there was a suspicious absence of behavioral science in the curriculum. In the meantime, other schools had incorporated more of a behavioral-science emphasis and considered it important. Their ironic recommendation was to mount a major recruiting effort to obtain top-talent behavioral-science faculty to reenergize the curriculum.

UNDERSTANDING THE CYCLICAL NATURE OF POWER DISTRIBUTIONS WITHIN ORGANIZATIONS

Power is distributed in organizations according to the externally controlled elements of the firm's environment. How power is allocated among lateral units, and for that matter, among individuals in the firm representing those units, is a function of how the firm's problems are defined according to the external contingencies the firm faces. The people who head up the units that will most likely solve the firm's problems—the units the firm is most dependent upon for its survival—accrue power. This power in turn creates the internal power distribution of the firm.

This knowledge is fundamental to understanding how to approach, and solve, problematic lateral relationships. In fact, knowledge of how power is distributed in your firm is so critical to your ability to get things done that you must learn quickly how to recognize the hallmarks of power. This requires taking a macroview of your organization, understanding what critical contingencies it currently faces, and mapping a pathway though the politics of your firm in a way that enhances rather than diminishes your goals. It is surprising how few people actually perform this type of analysis or take the time to understand who it is that holds the scarce and critical resources within their firms.

THE ECONOMIC-CONSULTING FIRM CASE

The example of the economic-analysis consulting firm case illustrates why understanding power distributions is so important. To understand this case, we must first acquaint you with the nature of work in consulting firms.

Most consulting firms are set up in a triad organizational design, such that the recent M.B.A.s and Ph.D.s are at the bottom of the pyramid, where the real work of the firm gets done. Associates are in the middle of the pyramid; their job is to supervise ongoing project assignments and assemble project teams of grunts and analysts. Partners at the top go golfing. Because a junior associate's reputation is built on his or her ability to assemble a terrific working team, personnel selection decisions are critical.

At this particular well-known economic-analysis firm, a decision was made to expand its staff. The president of the firm set up a committee consisting of six individuals to head up this expansion. Three of the committee members were partners, and the other three were junior associates. One of those junior associates was Mark. To fill one particular position, the committee sorted through dozens of resumes for weeks on end. Finally, after much thoughtful consideration, the committee selected six candidates.

All six finalists met the minimum and advertised criteria for the job positions—criteria that the committee members had agreed upon a priori as being the critical considerations for new hires. All agreed that three of the candidates were better than the other three. But for the remaining three candidates, the committee members could not make a clear choice as to who was the front runner.

Mark dutifully performed his analysis of the candidates, and it was clear to him that the preferential candidate was a male applicant from Stanford University. However, one of the senior partners preferred a woman from Georgetown University. They argued considerably but could not convince each other of the alternative point of view. Mark felt the older gentleman only wanted the woman because he thought he would be better able to boss around a woman than a man. The person being hired, however, was going to be working directly for the senior partner. Except for these two candidates, the other members of the committee were indifferent. Logically, both met the criteria for the job (recent Ph.D.s in economics, a knowledge of econometrics and statistics, and facility with a PC), so any choice was arbitrary in many respects.

Upon hearing the elements of this case, many new managers analyze the problem in terms of the young turk's lack of authority. They suggest a simplistic remedy: to convince those with authority on the merits of your favored job candidate. Such was the strategy undertaken in this case. Mark pleaded with the older partner about the merits of his favored candidate, but to no avail.

Mark's next approach was to discuss the merits of his candidate with those who were lateral to him—the junior associates—to get their support. He lobbied them about the merits of the male from Stanford versus the woman from Georgetown, and they all agreed that clearly Mark had a point. So at the next meeting, in front of the senior partners, Mark made his case for his favored candidate once again. Surprisingly, the coalition of support he thought he had assembled in the hallways suddenly and suspiciously disappeared.

It was clear to everyone but Mark that the power coalition within the firm favored the older partner's assessment. This was not because the older partner had performed a more intricate analysis or for some reason unknown to Mark, the male candidate had some specialized knowledge the firm needed. The reason the older gentleman's recommendation was favored was because he was a partner and held long-time associations with key clients who were important to the firm's portfolio. If he wanted to work with the male candidate, so be it. His opinion ruled because he held a resource that was vital to the firm's operation—power—and everyone but Mark was too wise to go against him.

ASSESSING POWER DISTRIBUTIONS

It is for this reason that assessing the power distributions of a firm is so important. Knowledge about the internal power distribution of the firm would have helped Mark keep his mouth shut so that he would not have found himself in such a political morass. In fact, it is important to learn quickly how to recognize how power is distributed in your firm to avoid making mistakes like Mark's. Without this knowledge, you may find that you fall flat on your face when you attempt to introduce your next great idea.

If you were Mark, it would have been helpful for you to assess the power distribution in advance. The most effective strategy we recommend for assessing power distributions in organizations is to look very hard and carefully at the environment of your firm to determine the kinds of critical problems the firm faces currently. Organizations face problems with demand at one time in their history and at other times it may be supply problems. Remember, power is cyclical. Once you have a handle on this, you should then be able to anticipate the kinds of talents that are going to be useful in solving those problems. What units are likely to be growing to help the firm survive? That's where you want to be.

Let's attempt to identify the underlying power distribution at a firm to illustrate this strategy. Let's say that you work at a major technology-driven firm such as Hewlett Packard. To identify the power distribution that underlies such a firm, you must first ask the question, What is their business? Reflecting upon this question a moment, you may answer that Hewlett Packard primarily is in the computer and calculator business. They also sell medical equipment and a few other lines of business.

The next question to ask is, Where do they make most of their money? You may answer that it may be in their printers, which are unequaled, and their medical equipment, which is considered top-notch.

This leads to the next question, How do they convince hospitals to purchase their medical equipment and professors and business people to purchase their computers and printers? By producing excellence in their products, you may answer. Hewlett Packard is a company that has a long tradition of technical excellence.

Now we can get somewhere in our analysis. The next question is, What is critical for their survival? If Hewlett Packard's reason for existing is to produce top-notch technical equipment, then a very critical resource becomes the talent of the personnel hired to work for the firm. If lousy engineers are hired, then lousy products are produced. But if engineering geniuses are hired, the company can really get somewhere.

Therefore engineering expertise is critical to their survival in their industry's corporate jungle. They have a reputation for engineering excellence. So they set up very tight relationships with schools like Stanford, MIT, and CalTech. They recruit and recruit and recruit. Now the next question is, How do they attract the best and the brightest? What do they do that's special?

This is a fundamental question because it gets at the essence of the firm's dependence on the most critical resource that is necessary for its survival. They need creative talent, and they need good technical talent. They need people who can manage technical types, and they need technical stars. They must find a way to get these brilliant, creative, energetic engineers to come to work for them and work their heads off. So what do they provide as the carrot?

They provide freedom, which for an engineer is probably the most important thing. Engineers are not necessarily in their professions to make money. What they want is toys to play with. They are turned on by design projects. They like to invent. They like to see how things work. They like to build things, dismantle them, and then start all over again.

The critical resource that engineers want from a firm is the opportunity to have fun with a whole series of exciting, new, and creative projects. They also want options. So Hewlett Packard provides a multitude of toys that these professionals can play with and offers opportunities galore. They provide flexible work hours that allow the engineers to work on a variety of projects in a variety of ways. They pay their best people well. They also offer a dual career track so that you don't have to get into management to be paid well. What more could an engineer want? Such a company, bursting with opportunities, is a dream come true.

BUDGETARY AND STRUCTURAL ANALYSIS

When looked at this way, you can see that it is a very simple matter to understand how power distributions in firms are created. Another way to understand the power distribution of a firm is to get a sense of the size of the budgets of the major units and subunits of the firm. You may think that the size of a subunit's budget is private information. This may be true. But an estimate or idea of a department's budget can be determined in a number of creative ways. One way that one of the authors of this book has discovered has considerable reliability and validity is to simply look at the telephone directory of your firm.

Most firms have telephone directories. Besides all the names and numbers, telephone directories contain considerable useful information. In addition to a listing of names, these directories typically have departmental listings for ease in finding a person you may wish to call. You may discover, for example, that the engineering department has eighteen inches of persons. When you compare that to the marketing department, you discover that marketing only has six inches of persons listed. What might this information tell you about the power distribution of the firm? This very simple artifact depicts that the firm employs seventy or so engineers and about twenty marketing professionals. What would you conclude about these department's budgets relative to one another? At this very basic level, we infer that the engineering department has a budget that outweighs that of marketing.

Another way you can get a sense of the current power distribution of a firm is to see how the firm structures itself. In addition to whether it has a big marketing department or a small marketing department, you can also look at whether it has a well-differentiated marketing department. For some firms, marketing and sales are the same thing. In other firms, marketing is understood to be of a more complex nature. They have a promotion department. They have a pricing unit. They have a high-end customer sales force and "average" sales force. They have a consumer-behavior research department. They have all kinds of subunits that are related to the knowledge of marketing and the available technologies for marketing pursuits. You can take a marketing textbook and see all the categories that go into marketing represented on the organizational chart. From that you can see how well differentiated marketing can be. Now look at the production unit and the financial unit. Are they as well differentiated as the marketing groups? If not, what does this tell you about the power distribution of the firm?

It is also helpful to analyze the interdependencies among departments. Those departments that interact and transact most frequently with other departments are likely to be perceived in the departmental pecking order as most critical. What are those departments? Visit as many departments as possible. Ask how its work fits into the work of the others. Get to know as many people as you can across departments. Anytime there is an assignment that crosses departments, take it. You will increase your mobility in the organization if your work is viewed as important to more than one area.

HISTORICAL ANALYSIS

You also should examine how power has shifted over time as part of your analysis. Sometimes organizations or departments simply won't change, implement, innovate, or create, despite all of the best intentions. Sometimes the firm is stuck in the past. Why this happens has frustrated many a manager, but the reason is not really so baffling. In short, many of today's organizations were "born" at a time when a different managerial or organizational paradigm ruled. That is, many of our industrial and even service organizations began around the turn of the century—the boom time for American urbanization and industrialization. During this time period, the overarching need was efficiency, resulting in the paradigm of scientific management. This paradigm rewarded efficiency and one best way to do things. Following scientific management came administrative management, with its emphasis on division of labor, rules, policies, and bureaucratic structures. The most recent paradigm has been team management, resulting from corporations' need to globalize their units and operate in a more decentralized manner.

Although we have attempted to change these paradigms, the thinking and ways of doing things that underlie them remains deeply entrenched. Over the past fifteen years, changing structures has been one of the most dominant organizational activities. Nevertheless, many firms seem to have changed on the surface, but a deeply entrenched culture continues to dominate.

To understand the historical nature of the paradigms that affect your firm's culture, first look for trends. One way to do this is to find a talkative member of the organization who has been around for awhile and who has perhaps seen thirty years worth of change in the firm. What trends can be identified? Are those trends cyclical? Do certain departments periodically rise to the forefront as changes in the external environment occur? What have been the major crisis events that have precipitated internal changes of reorganization and priorities? What has the fallout been from such crises?

An interesting way to look at these issues is to view the tenure of each successive corporate operating officer to understand what the issues were under his or her reign. Each senior officer was promoted at a time to solve a key organizational problem. When product quality is lousy, engineers are promoted. When financial indicators fall, financial people are promoted. When markets change, marketing people are promoted. Chances are there are key crisis events that precipitated each executive's tenure in the position. Identify what those events were to see if you can discern a pattern. In hospitals, for example, most current CEOs have come from the ranks of finance, frequently working their way up as chief financial officers. This is not surprising, given how financial concerns have dominated the health-care arena over the past few decades. Second in power in most hospitals is the legal department. This is again a historical change—a few decades ago hospitals generally consulted an externally housed lawyer only when crisis situations arose. Both the increase in malpractice as well as the increase in regulatory bodies dictating hospital protocols have spurred the rise of internal legal departments.

In fact, an analysis of the backgrounds and historical facts concerning corporate officers can yield considerable information. Look at their educational and firm experience. Generally this is public information, but sometimes it is easiest to find it out simply by talking with people. Almost all organizations have traditional places where they recruit. Some organizations require an Ivy League degree. Others insist on engineering schools. Still others hire locally. Look and see who gets promoted in the firm. There is a tendency in organizations, once the educational criteria are met, that people move up the corporate ladder from certain departments or certain areas of experience. In the economic consulting firm case, for example, all of the players arose through that organization from the government-research department. Research was a very important area of that firm. In another firm it may be required, for example, that you do a tour of duty in the field as a plant manager. Are you willing to do that? Or perhaps you must relocate overseas to be considered for the really plum assignments back home. These are some things you can understand a priori, if you really look.

CULTURAL–ANTHROPOLOGICAL ANALYSIS

With your anthropological hat on, it is also possible to assess power distributions within a firm by examining what has been referred to as the symbols of power. Who has the big corner office? Who plays golf with the CEO? Who had no difficulty whatsoever putting through that major computer order while others grovel for one additional piece of equipment? Who has the best office furniture? Who gets to eat in the executive dining room? Which groups have better access to trivial resources? Who are the people that everyone likes to tell stories about? What symbols of power are important? The trouble with this strategy is that typically, at the highest levels of the firm, all the executives have these symbols, but not all of them have equivalent power. But, at the lower levels, this type of analysis may yield some interesting information. Depending on your willingness to risk being rude, you could simply ask, Who's got the power around here?

A better approach may be to have lunch in the company cafeteria to get the scuttlebutt about what it takes to be successful in the organization. Ask for views about promotion criteria. What kinds of experiences are necessary and where? Is line experience helpful? International experience? Strategic planning experience? Marketing experience? Who is considered high potential and why? What kinds of agreements are generated if you are? What if you are not? Who are the bosses to work for and why? What jobs should you stay away from? What are considered to be the dead-end assignments? Which departments are dead-ends? Typically these are the units that have very flat hierarchies and limited opportunities for advancement and employ specialists whose expertise is not needed elsewhere in the firm.

As part of your lunchroom discussions, you may want to ask people what happened the last time they proposed a new project. Ask how difficult it was to get approval for new projects. What are the chains of decisions that must be made? Who holds authority over such decisions? What conflicts are created by new projects that are being proposed? The conflicts you unearth will tell you that power organizes around the issues presented in the conflict.

Finally, you should examine the process of how decisions are made to understand how the work is getting done. Most firms do a lot of work through committees. Some committees in firms are important, while others are not very important. Some are standing committees or permanent committees, while others are temporary ad-hoc committees. Usually the committees that have money attached to them are the important committees. Personnel committees, executive compensation committees, budgeting committees, and any committee that has approval over the important organizational decisions are the ones to watch. What you must do is to find out who sits on these committees. Find out the nature of these persons, where they come from, and what kind of talent basis or what kind of department experience they have. This type of analysis often yields useful information.

USING POWER DISTRIBUTIONS
TO UNDERSTAND POLITICS

What we are offering are some ideas of how to go about analyzing the power distribution and the political climate of the firm. It is surprising to us how few people actually perform this sort of analysis and it is shocking to us how many people, like Mark from the economic consulting firm case, seem blindsighted when political realities hit them in the face. They then wonder why they don't seem to fit on the firm's coveted career paths.

The reason they are misfits is that most often they have not yet taken the time to analyze their capabilities versus the organization's needs. They know they are good. They know they are intelligent. They know they should be getting somewhere. But they assume there is a linear relationship between the merits of their performance and eventual career advancement, which simply does not exist. One's advancement in a firm is instead based on a curvilinear relationship that ebbs and flows according to the political winds of power. It is for this reason that the study of power distributions in organizations and their political and cultural realities and ramifications is so very important.

3

Determining Your Resources
in the New Lateral Organization

Consider the case of a young woman who wanted to get into the Labor and Industrial Relations (LIR) School at a prestigious Ivy League university. In December, when Connie received her GRE scores in the mail, she was disappointed to learn that her quantitative scores were below the minimum for acceptance. She had already applied to the LIR School when her scores arrived. Connie had heard so many good things about the LIR School that she desperately wanted to be admitted; as far as she was concerned, the LIR School was the only pathway to her future career.

From the foregoing analyses of externally controlled power distributions in firms, what would you recommend Connie do in this situation? The first step would be to perform an external-control analysis of this organization's environment. The external environment of an organization like this brings up several questions. How does a university make its money? It does so by attracting a qualified pool of applicants who are willing to pay tuition dollars for educational services. What attracts a qualified pool of applicants? A good reputation is necessary. How are university reputations created? One medium is the printed word—what evaluators in the news media write about the quality of the educational programs offered. The other medium is what people say about the school. Most schools develop their reputations from the success of their graduates. Their success attracts prospective students. The quality of the current student body also enhances the reputation of the schools.

Therefore, the word-of-mouth discussions of former students, current students, and prospective students that come into contact with the school are very critical to disbursing information that creates and maintains the school's reputation. It is vital for a quality school like this to maintain its reputation. Understanding this fact is central to the power analysis of this firm. If Connie wishes to increase her chances of acceptance, it would be in her best interest to visit the school in person, at whatever personal cost, to plead her case.

It turns out that the way admissions decisions are made in most schools is through a three-tiered selection process. Applications are randomly assigned to admissions staff who sort through and select the most compelling candidates who fit the criteria. Those candidates not selected—who may have good qualities but do not fit the criteria as easily—are then reviewed in a roundtable discussion. Finally, the total pool is reviewed for overall demographics and additional selections are made.

This means that if Connie misses out on the first round of admissions, which is quite likely with her low quantitative scores, she may gain a second chance midway through the process. Her chances of admission are greatly increased if she is able to influence the admissions director to consider her. What resource does Connie hold that the admissions director may appreciate?

Connie is from a mixed racial background of Indian, African American, and Creole history. Connie's most recent job involved public relations work for a large industrial manufacturer. With this information in place, what do you think Connie's chances for admission will be if she visits the school in person? How should she plead her case?

Connie was dependent on the admissions director of the school to consider accepting her despite her low quantitative scores. But she too had resources to use as levers in the situation. Her own resources included her racial background and her work accomplishments. Connie highlighted these aspects of her background in her interview. You can bet her comments made an impression on the admissions director, who was dutifully impressed.

This case illustrates the fact that there is a fundamental relationship that exists between those parties that are in power and those that are not. This relationship's concerns, surprisingly, are your dependences on others.

POWER–DEPENDENCE RELATIONS

In 1962, a sociologist by the name of Richard Emerson published a largely unheralded paper in the *American Sociological Review* titled "Power–Dependence Relations." He defined a fundamental truth that applies to all social relationships: that power and dependence are inversely related. Individuals hold power over others to the degree that others are dependent on them for a resource they need to achieve the goals they desire. Simply stated, when you need something from someone else, that person holds power over you. Conversely, you hold power if someone depends on you for some resource that they need.

Lateral relationships in organizations follow this basic premise. When you are trying to get specialized equipment from one department to better serve your own, you are dependent on a peer within that department to give you the OK. When you hit a brick wall while shepherding a major planning initiative, you are dependent on the good will of other lateral peers to convince the naysayers why your initiative should be followed. When your job has been reorganized, your latest good idea will go nowhere unless you obtain the resources you need to accomplish your goals.

In fact, much of our lives are structured around power–dependence relations. In corporate life, our relationships are structured so that we are dependent on bosses for promotions, favorable performance ratings, or raises to buy new cars. We are dependent on peers for information critical to our jobs. We are dependent on outside suppliers to supply us with the resources that we deem necessary to manufacture the products or provide the services that are our purpose in the first place. As bosses we are dependent on our employees to perform their work effectively and efficiently so that we can look good to the "higher-ups" and get promoted ourselves.

Dependency relations organize social relationships and explain why power is so problematic. When you are dependent on someone, the person who holds what you need has the power in that particular social relation because he or she has discretion to provide what you need in response to your requests. What is so interesting to note here is that the basic fundamental truth of why someone holds power over you— the structure of the social relation—is because you believe you depend on that person for something that you think you need. In other words, we create other's power.

Their power arises from our perceived dependency on them for some resource. For example, the power a professor has over her students has little to do with their influence or rights. Instead, it has everything to do with the student's dependence in that social relation. The only reason the professor holds power over students is because the professor controls a valued commodity: grades. This situation has nothing to do with the love of learning or respect for authority. It has everything to do with the resource at hand.

Now if a student in a class does not care about his grade, then the professor has limited power, and therefore can only remotely influence his behavior. If he chooses not to show up for class, there is little the professor can do. But if another student desperately wants a good grade, perhaps because the course is in her major and she is failing everything else, then the professor will hold considerable power in that social relation. The professor can use her influence to easily convince the latter student to serve as an unpaid student research assistant, while the former student would not consider such a request.

RESOURCES AS SOCIAL CONSTRUCTIONS

The mechanism that underlies such relationships is the need for a resource that you believe you need that someone else holds. In the case of a teacher–student relationship, it is easy to see that the teacher holds dominion over the student's grade. But in life there are many resources for which we allow ourselves to be dependent.

What is a resource? Anything can be a resource, and the specifics about what is and what is not a resource are not important. Money is generally thought to be a resource, only because people are willing to trade for it. But there are many other resources as well. Information is a key organizational resource. Access to fun and exciting job assignments can also be considered a resource. Job security can be a resource. Love and attention can be as well.

Resources are often taken to be substantial material things and events, and this leads many people to misunderstand what their true capabilities are in a power–dependence relation. In our view, a resource is a socially constructed object that depends for its very meaning on the ideological beliefs that function in a dependency relationship. By implication, a resource is not defined and has no meaning outside of the role it plays in the interdependency between the two lateral parties. If one person has a capability that serves the other's desire, then that capability is a resource. Otherwise, it is not. A valuable resource is simply the capability of one person believed to be serviceable for fulfilling the desires of others. Thus, if a professor's ability to give a student a high grade on a paper were not something the student desired, not to mention their parents and future employers, then this ability would have little meaning. Grades are only resources because they are socially constructed as such.

But resources are socially constructed in a more important way as well. The capabilities that underlie them are frequently generated through a social process or through social institutions. Thus, the ability of the professor to give grades to students is not as a result of the astonishing physical or mental abilities of the professor, it is simply a capability any human has who can write the appropriate letters or numbers used to represent grades. However, an institution evolved which served to underlie the relationship between the student and the professor. These institutions and their supporting ideologies uniquely ascribe meaning to the professor's scribbling, consequently denying it to all others.

Basically, a resource gains its status from the role it plays in a social relationship. A resource is any capability that plays a role in a social relationship. If you have the capability to dispense bonus money at the end of the year to your employees, then bonus money could be considered a resource in that particular social relation. But what if one of your employees—the one whom you are most trying to motivate— is independently wealthy? Then providing bonus monies to him or her at year's end isn't going to go far. This is why resource dependence is defined precisely by the nature of the relationship and the desires of the less powerful party in the social relation.

When we want to get promoted, admitted to a school, or gain a favorable work assignment, we have desires that make us dependent. Such desires are socially constructed. The reason in the first place that we might wish to be promoted is to get more money. Money in our society has been deemed a good thing to have. It allows us to trade in all kinds of goods that may support a chosen lifestyle. But if you do not wish to have more money, then you are not dependent on your boss to support you for that promotion. Perhaps you can live a spartan existence quite as happily as a moneyed one.

Our desires are socially constructed because there are things in life we are supposed to have. If you don't have something you want, you perceive that someone else has what you want. You believe that your boss has the ability to provide you with more money to support an enhanced lifestyle, whether he does or doesn't. But you must believe this to be true to be caught in a dependency relation with him in the first place.

Furthermore, you must perceive that you lack alternatives to gain the resource you need. You must not have won the lottery recently. Your parents must not have left you a large inheritance. You must have chosen not to work two jobs. You must have chosen not to be a high-stakes drug dealer on the side. As we stated earlier, there are always alternatives. The question is whether you choose to accept them and put them into action.

Finally, you must believe that the other party upon whom you are dependent has the discretion to determine whether to support your cause. This other party's discretion is socially controlled by his or her acceptance of the context of the social relation. If your boss argues that you cannot be promoted at the present time because there is a promotion and hiring freeze, then so be it. You must accept his words. Or must you?

Much of what dependence is founded upon is in the eye of the beholder. Our powerlessness in social relations is built upon a flimsy edifice of our own perceptions, needs, and desires, which is to say that a lot of these relationships are basically mythological. If we choose not to believe that we have alternatives, we lock ourselves into a dependence relation. If we accept the constraints presented by the context, then we allow ourselves to be rendered powerless.

The truth is that every key element of interdependent relations between two parties is subject to and part of the politics of their relationship. Every element is open to creation, manipulation, fabrication, definition, and most important, social construction. This is why lateral relationships in organizations are so problematic. Every element of a lateral relationship is subject to social negotiation and redefinition. In upward relationships, there are often social caveats that govern these relationships, such as, "Thou shalt not speak to thy boss's boss unless thou has thy boss's permission first." In lateral relationships, on the other hand, anything goes.

USING RESOURCES TO YOUR ADVANTAGE

The fact that lateral relationships are less well defined than boss–employee relationships, makes them more problematic, in that there are less social caveats to follow. However, they also can work to your advantage. It is important to remember that your dependence in social relationships is a two-way street, in that by definition there are two parties who are involved in the social relationship. The professor is dependent on the students, though for different resources. The student can offer to the professor the resource of his or her time to serve as an unpaid research assistant. Time in academe is a very valuable commodity. And bosses are dependent on their employees to perform their work excellently and on time so that they look good in front of higher-ups.

The key point here is that when you are in a dependent relationship, there may be some resources you hold that the more powerful member may wish to trade in exchange for what you want. A professor may find a letter from you complimenting his or her performance, written to the dean at a time when the professor is being evaluated for promotion, to be a valuable resource. Your boss may view your willingness to work on a project that he has been unable to give his time and attention to as a valuable resource. A peer in another department may give you angst when you want to install a new, improved computer program, but may look favorably upon your work when you show her installing the program will cut her workload in half.

We believe that often the reason why people fail to manage their lateral relationships effectively is because they don't take the time to understand the reverse dependencies that govern those relationships. Before we can manage, direct, influence, or even fully cooperate with people in lateral relationships, we must comprehend the flip side of dependence.

Ask yourself, What can I offer in exchange for the resource I want to receive? What does this person value? It may be money, it may be time, it may be approval or respect, or it may be visibility, recognition, or the smooth sailing of a recent initiative. Chances are, what he or she values will be directly in line with the critical resources, as defined by the current state of organization. This returns us to an understanding of the power distribution of the organization, as controlled by external environmental factors that the firm currently faces. We refer to this as the context or background of the power–dependence relationship.

UNDERSTANDING CONTEXT IN
POWER–DEPENDENCE RELATIONSHIPS

What is context? *Webster's* tells us one definition is "a necessary accompaniment or necessary link." This goes beyond knowing what business or task the organization, department, or individual unit is engaged in; it involves being cognizant of the resources and dependencies of the people whose support we need or whom we seek to influence. This is the necessary link.

Relationship "failures" occur when managers think they know the context, when what they know is what business their firms are engaged in. The context involves understanding what makes the organization tick—what it is fundamentally dependent upon to survive.

If you can do a resource diagnosis of the context, ideally, before you act, then you have a greater chance of successfully accomplishing your goal. It will be easier to present and gain acceptance for your idea because your idea will be in line with and will support organizational goals. Whether or not an idea or objective gets accepted has everything to do with the perceived resource needs of the firm, which is based on what is critical to the firm's survival at the moment.

Getting to this understanding involves more than interpersonal skills. Sometimes, managers think they have a pretty good handle on the "interpersonal skills" needed to govern human relationships. But uncovering resources and the interests behind them goes beyond interpersonal or intuitive skills. Awareness of the resource needs should be more carefully attended and more accurately diagnosed via a tool we deem a "resource analysis."

Performing a Resource Analysis

A resource analysis is a systematic diagnosis that can be applied to any department or organization. A resource analysis involves asking certain fundamental questions. It combines some of the concepts we mention in Chapter 2 as the resource analysis will be shaped by the cultural and historical forces that will in turn shape the current power distribution of the firm.

To perform a resource analysis, we want to understand

1. What the firm or department is dependent upon.
2. Who manages those fundamental dependencies.
3. Who is important in the organization, beyond title and rank.
4. How and why power is distributed the way it is.
5. The communication networks that govern this management.

Resources are, simply put, what the organization needs to conduct its business. As we discussed earlier, they can be tangible or intangible. For a university, for example, resources of students, faculty, physical plant, technology, and dollars are important. Less tangible resources include such things as reputation and networks for communication, both internal among the people and external, toward alumni and the media. In a consulting firm, the clients and the relationships that manage the clients are the fundamental and critical resources.

To perform a resource analysis, we recommend that you consider the following questions:

1. Think about the resources your department or organization depends upon.
2. Write down as many resources as you can think of, separating them into two columns of "tangible," such as money and specific people, and "less tangible," such as skills and reputation. The reason for this is that we are accustomed to thinking about tangible resources such as money and physical items, and more recently, people. However, resources also include the intangible, such as reputation and information.
3. Next, determine which of these resources are absolutely critical for the organization or department's survival. In the case of LIR, we might say the students, faculty, and dollars are the most critical resources. Other aspects are important, to be sure, but the university could not survive without students, faculty, and dollars. At a consulting firm, the critical resources are relationships, reputation, information, and people, and more specifically the partners and the associates who manage the client relationships.
4. Write down how these resources are managed. Why does the university continue to have students and money, for example? You might well determine that reputation is why students continue to come to the school. It may be equally true that the reputation of the students, as well as the jobs they obtain also contribute to the ongoing reputation. The faculty manage reputation. And, more than ever, the media helps to manage reputation, with indicators such as *Business Week* and college guides and a

seemingly endless stream of popular-press ranking reports. In the consulting firm example, why does the firm continue to exist? The resources of reputation, clients, and the relationships that manage them are in the hands of the partners and associates. This is why attempting to implement a plan that bypasses or in any way diminishes the power of the partners and associates is impossible, as in the economic consulting firm case.

5. Now, write down who manages these critical resources. Although this is sometimes similar to question four of how the resources are managed, it is useful to ask who in order to be sure you understand who holds the powerful positions. Sometimes it is not the person in authority.

6. Have certain resources become more scarce for the organization in recent years? If so, list which resources have become more scarce and difficult to obtain. There is a relationship between scarcity and perceived value. That is, if student enrollments, for example, decline and that resource has been counted as critical to the organization's survival, the role, function, and ultimately the people who manage enrollment become all the more vital. That is why student-affairs departments and the position of dean of student affairs has in many schools become a more important entity in the past five years than the deans of faculty departments are. If we were to consider a consulting firm in health care, it would be important to note that legal departments and financial departments have become more important in recent years, as legal and policy issues and management have become increasingly vital and finances increasingly constrained.

7. Look at your list of nontangibles, such as reputation. Universities survive and thrive based very much on reputation, especially when competition for students is keen. If we analyze how those reputations are managed, we realize why such indicators as *Business Week*'s rankings of colleges and universities has become so important to schools. You might realize that the public-relations department (which ten years ago may have been a part-time position) has become prominent in universities, and the people who manage PR have become increasingly powerful in a setting that historically has disdained their influence. This is why Connie's use of the resource she had at her disposal was so vital to her admissions decision. Public relations would have viewed her admission as a necessary and important step in increasing the diversity of their student body and could have influenced the admissions director to allow her admission.

The Promise of Resource Analysis

Using these questions to analyze the resources available at your disposal within lateral relationships will help you to gain advantage in those relationships where you find yourself in the more dependent, powerless position. Remember, power is cyclical. It ebbs and flows based on external critical contingencies.

The power balance within lateral relationships is therefore determined by how players act within the social relationship: (1) defining what resources are important and (2) developing control over scarce resources. By understanding and identifying which resources are most important, you can begin the process of developing an action plan to achieve your goal.

According to Emerson, two properties create one's dependence on another party for a resource: (1) You have no other alternatives for that resource, and (2) you are motivationally invested in achieving your goal. In other words, your desires create your dependence on others. Also, in your view, no one else has exactly the right capability to provide what you need. This was Connie's problem. She wanted to go to the LIR School because she knew it was the best in the country. She saw herself as having no other alternatives that matched the prestige and reputation of the LIR School. Her motivational investment was high. She made herself dependent.

Dependence is subjectively created and externally controlled. It is subjectively created because you believe in your heart that you need the resource that you seek. It is externally controlled because you lack capacity for that resource, and you must go elsewhere to get it. In order to understand these principles in action, it is necessary to examine the anatomy of a dependency relationship.

4

The ABC Paradigm as an Organizing Model

The goal of this book is to demonstrate how to manage power in lateral relationships. So far, we have argued that lateral relationships can be better managed if the resources and dependencies that undergird them are more clearly understood. We have said that this is not a haphazard affair, but rather something we can and should be comfortable with as part of our understanding of the ebb and flow of business.

In the next three chapters, we will be looking at a model that brings lateral relationships into sharper relief. It is a model for analyzing, diagnosing, and "seeing" political relationships. We have used this model to diagnose all manner of political relationships in which our M.B.A. students and our clients have found themselves in their firms. It is called the "ABC" model, because we have sought to create a simple model that is applicable to virtually any lateral relationship in which one party wants or needs something from another. Our students and clients report that by diagramming the lateral relationships, they "see" the situation in a way that gives them new insights into the nature of the target, their own goals, and the existence of viable options for action. In these three chapters, we demonstrate the heart of effective action planning for managing lateral relationships.

In this chapter, we begin with the basic anatomy of dependency relationships. We then turn to the set of strategies available to any agent. These strategic options are discussed at length in Chapter 5. By examining strategic options, agents can determine strategic game plans to affect the various components of the lateral relationship. Detailed action planning, including the caveats for planning political action, is the blueprint of Chapter 6.

Our anatomy of dependency relations begins with an understanding that there are three central aspects which exist in all dependency relationships. These aspects include A, which is the agent of the relationship who desires a resource; B, the target of the power–dependence relationship and the one who holds the resource; and X, the objective or resource desired.

Say that A, the agent, wants something, and that A is dependent on B, the target, for some reason. The problem is that A wants a resource that B holds and A does not have the capacity or capability to achieve it on his or her own. A must also believe that B has the capability to provide what he or she needs. What is necessary and important here is that the actor who wants something believes that there exists someone who does have that ability.

B also is endowed with certain properties. B has the capability to provide what A wants. These capabilities can be anything. What matters is that both actors are willing to trade in that capability, whatever it may be. The fact is that A wants to achieve a particular goal, such as a promotion, and believes that B can help him or her achieve it. A then also establishes an instrumental relationship with B, with the purpose of helping him achieve that goal. With the instrumentality of the relationship in hand, A has made himself or herself dependent on B for the goal or resource sought. For purposes of convenience, we will name the resource X. In the LIR admissions case in Chapter 3, Connie is dependent on the director for admission to the school, despite her lack of qualifications. Her wish to be admitted is the X, or the objective.

Power is derived from these dependencies. The power of B is the converse of A's dependency on B. A has basically now granted to B power over him or her by virtue of this social relationship. Largely what causes dependency or powerlessness is your own desires. If you are dependent on someone, and if that dependency is destructive in some way or simply not favorable to you, and you wish to get out of it, keep in mind that you are the one that produced it in the first place by your own whims and desires. One of the things that we will examine is that there is a kind of political contest that emerges around the desires and wants that human beings have. From the point of view of B, it is in B's interest to get A to believe that everything A wants B has the ability to provide. It is for this reason that people frequently try to control others' desires.

Analyze, for a moment, a love relationship. Love relationships are defined in such a way that there is only one supplier who will meet your desires. In other words, there is only one person on earth that knocks your socks off and makes your heart pound. However, in life, there are always other Bs. There are always other suppliers in any dependency situation. There are other persons similar to B out there in the world with whom you might fall in love if you allowed it to happen. There are other persons in the organization who might aid your desires to get promoted.

The trouble is, we often fail to recognize the alternative Bs of the situation. The other Bs in fact do exist, but you choose to frame the situation so that the other Bs are not as attractive as your number-one B. In Connie's situation, there were other schools available. But Connie was not willing to consider other schools. She framed the situation such that she was solely dependent on the decision made by the admissions director of her first-choice school.

The magnitude or extent of an agent's dependency on a target actor is partly a function of the number of alternatives that are available, as well as a function of how badly the agent wants the resource or goal in the first place. In general, the more alternatives there are, the less dependent you are. You may begin to notice here that framing is critical. How you define the relationship also is key. Frequently this is the trouble with love relationships; you define your desires or your needs in such a way that there is only one supplier. This also is true of career brick walls; you define the situation in such a way that you must stay in your current firm in your current department for some reason or another, and you believe you have no alternatives to pursue.

There is a second element of this relationship that deserves note. B has been endowed with discretion. The admissions director has discretion to help Connie or not. B can always do nothing about your request. B does not have to satisfy your whims. The admissions director has choices about how he will fill the remaining places. B has freedom of action. B can allocate coveted resources any way he or she wishes. This means that your promotion can easily go to your arch enemy, or the love of your life may suddenly decide to pursue his or her own romantic interests elsewhere.

It is important to understand the attributes of the A, B, C, and X relationship, because this forms the model for all lateral relationships in which something is wanted. These attributes are as follows:

A. The agent	has discretion.
	has a desire or need.
	believes a target exists who can provide what is needed or wanted.
B. The target	has discretion.
	has a resource needed (or perceived to be needed by agent).
C. The context	norms, rules, culture, or regulation forms the context of the A–B relationship.

X. The desire	the need, want, or goal held by A.
A1. Alternate agents	also wants a resource from B, and so may be in competition with the agent.
B1. Alternate targets	other targets or potential targets who may be capable of granting A's request.

THE ALL IMPORTANT CONTEXT

There is a third element, the context, or C, which regulates the relationship between A and B. We use the word agent because a regulator may be a person, an organization, or an ideology. This regulatory agency may be an actor, such as a state, or an institution, such as a norm. It takes many forms, and its presence may be felt to a greater or lesser extent and attended to more or less often. The regulatory agent does not formally belong exclusively to the relationship between A and B, but is part of the context that regulates how they behave toward one another. The social context of the situation puts the central dependency relation into an externally controlled context.

One form of a regulator that can be clearly identified are any laws that exist which shape behavior. But regulatory agents need not be restricted to being only laws. Organizations and their rules, ideologies, mythologies, and systems of authority and supervision are also regulators. Policies that mandate who reports to whom in an organization or who may evaluate whom explicitly determine dependencies among its personnel. Even less commonly considered constructors of dependency relationships are the beliefs, assumptions, and definitions that parties have about one another and about themselves. An employee who believes the propaganda surrounding total quality management will be much easier to control than others who do not "buy in" to the latest scheme.

If you think about it, norms are very powerful regulators of social relationships, in that they effect most of your behavior in relationships. There are certain norms that exist now in your firm that control your behavior. There are norms about where you eat lunch. There are norms about working in teams rather than as individual contributors. There are norms about whether to have a problem addressed by the next level or solve it on your own. There are norms about asking outright for a raise. There are norms that organizations create to manage these kinds of situations and to keep them under control.

These kinds of norms are often so powerful and insidious that sometimes we accept them without question. Think for a moment how organizations control success. The culture of the firm defines success, and then the members of the firm control the mechanisms by which success is achieved. They dictate who performs well and who does not; whether you are a good employee or not; or whether you fit in or not. When you think about social norms as control mechanisms, you may realize how much your behavior is controlled by these norms. How you behave in a social situation is often a direct reflection of these norms. They exist to shape your desires and wants.

MARGARET AND THE BANK INFORMATION SYSTEM

Margaret was a newly hired M.B.A. at a large bank. The bank had recently acquired a number of smaller banks and was now the "flagship" or hub for the smaller, satellite banks. Margaret's position was assistant branch manager at the flagship bank. One of her key duties was to coordinate customer accounts. A time-consuming problem Margaret had observed was the lack of standardization among the bank's information systems.

Margaret's idea was to develop and implement a system for customer accounts that would standardize the information systems among all of the banks. Margaret worked on her plan for several months during her off time and, according to her calculations, determined her plan would save the bank several hundred thousands of dollars a year in coordination time. It would also eliminate the need for about a dozen personnel whose jobs involved coordinating the systems at the satellite banks. Margaret was very pleased with her work and presented it to her manager in a polished manner, complete with color charts and accurate financial data. She emphasized the cost savings and included a detailed implementation plan.

Margaret's branch manager reviewed the design for reengineering the bank information systems and put it aside with a curt note to Margaret informing her that both the plan and idea were inappropriate. Not to be discouraged, Margaret then took her plan to the vice president of operations, her manager's boss, certain that he would be impressed with the cost savings and detailed implementation plan. The vice president reprimanded Margaret and turned her proposal aside.

THE ABC MODEL APPLIED

The ABC theory considers power a part of the social relationship. It asserts that one party, B, has power over another, A, to the extent that A is dependent upon B (see Figure 4.1). In this example, Margaret is the agent, or A. Her boss is the target of the influence attempt, or B.

This model further asserts that A is dependent upon B, to the extent that A desires something and lacks the capability for fulfilling the desire on his or her own. In this example, Margaret wishes to put forth her standardization plan. This is something she cannot do on her own because she needs the support of her branch manager to accomplish her goal. Her boss, the branch manager, has the ability to give it the green light. To the extent that B is believed to have such ability and is

Figure 4.1
Actors in a Lateral Relationship and Their Attributes

X = What is wanted.

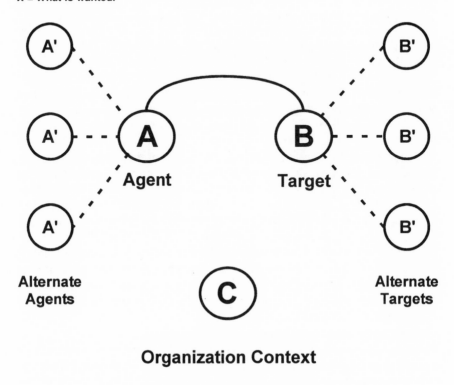

Organization Context

free and able to use that ability in the service of A's interests, A will depend upon B.

These are minimal and necessary conditions. But the extent of a dependency is further affected by the context within which the parties construct their relationship. This context is defined by three elements: alternatives for A, otherwise known as A primes; alternatives for B, otherwise known as B primes; and the third agency, C, or context. This is illustrated in Figure 4.1, which depicts a dependency relationship between A and B, in this case Margaret and her boss.

We know that Margaret wants her boss's approval to implement her new standardized information system. The resource that she wants, or X, is his approval. The way in which she decided to go about achieving X was to go to her boss and ask for his approval. When the resource she desired was not forthcoming, she went to the vice president of operations whom she defined in this case as an alternative B, or B prime. This only served to get her reprimanded for escalating the conflict.

How could this case have been solved without damage to Margaret's career? Let's look at the case from B's, or the boss's, perspective. Given the timing of the recent merger, the boss in this case is dependent upon smooth operating relationships within the new satellite banks. In other words, he does not want to rock the boat. The context in this case suggests caution. Further, his own power has increased within the incorporation, as now he has some three to four hundred employees reporting to him. He really doesn't want to kick a gift horse in the mouth, so to speak. Margaret is proposing to do exactly that.

Now let's look at this case from Margaret's perspective. The central question for Margaret is, What does she really want versus what does she need? As we said earlier, desires are socially constructed. She thinks she wants to establish a standardized information system. But what she really wants is respect, credibility for her actions, and the potential for future advancement. Upsetting her boss and his boss is clearly not the route to accomplish these goals.

Using the ABC paradigm, we can easily identify Margaret's dependence in this situation, which can help us devise a means of action that would be more productive than the route she chose. Four facts which can help to do this include the following:

1. A believes that A is dependent on B for a resource that B holds and can provide. In this case Margaret believes she is dependent on her boss for his approval of her plan.

2. B has a choice among the alternatives presented to him or her, such that B could choose to favor A, or another A prime. Margaret's boss could choose to support Margaret's plan, or could choose to favor the needs of the satellite banks, who are the A primes in this case.

3. A believes no competition exists, in that there are other B primes that A could identify who might provide the resource A seeks. Margaret tried to find a B prime. She thought she could go over her boss's head and convince another B of the worthiness of her implementation plan. She discovered this was not appropriate. This is C, the context of the organization, coming into play, suggesting there is a norm that Margaret broke.

4. B has discretion to favor A's position. Discretion is an absolute ability. It is an endowment and a property of being human. By implication, controlling a person's discretion is impossible. However, it may be possible to control how that person uses his or her endowment. That is, you might be able to influence a person's decisions about what to do—in particular, about whether to invest in your problems and needs. This returns us to an understanding and appreciation for C, the context of the situation. If the norms of the situation dictate that the timing isn't right, you shouldn't go over your boss's head, or that people who don't have a certain educational credential shouldn't be promoted, then it won't happen. This is true, unless exceptions are made. And that is where discretion comes full circle, and external control concepts come into play.

DIAGRAMMING LATERAL RELATIONSHIPS

We encourage managers to diagram the dependency relationship. When we look pictorially at the lateral relationships and the needs, context, and targets, it is literally easier to "see" what the relationship looks like and what levers can be affected. If we were to illustrate the lateral relationship in Margaret's case, it would look like Figure 4.2.

By diagramming the relationship, we can more clearly see the critical components of the network. We see who the agent's allies or competitors may be, in the form of other A primes who may seek similar or competing resources. We can more clearly state what the agent both wants and needs as X. We are compelled to more explicitly analyze C, the all important context, which is sometimes overlooked when well-meaning agents design action. Finally, by diagramming the ABC model, the agent may see not only the immediate target, but alternative targets. The alternative targets may hold the real power or have an important effect on the outcome. We advocate diagramming these targets because typically, they are are not as obvious to the agent.

One critical thing "seen" by diagramming the ABCs is the context. In this case, the context and specifically the timing were the elements that worked against Margaret's proposal, but she was blind to this. Also, Margaret made a classic mistake. She naively went over the boss's head, without realizing the particularly strong relationship between her boss and the vice president of operations in a context which dictated that underlings never go over the boss's head.

In the LIR example of Chapter 3, the admissions director's power was derived from the fact that extra places still existed in the final countdown for class space, that Connie believed that this was the only school for her, and that the admissions director could make a decision in her favor. Therefore, it became a simple matter for Connie to shape events in such a way that the admissions director would decide in her favor. In other words, Connie used the levers she had available to her to externally control the factors in the situation so that the admissions director would make a decision that favored her interests.

How B makes choices will be shaped by external control factors, or in other words, the factors in the situation that allow him or her to make a decision. A common model about decision making suggests that people make decisions after assessing all the available alternatives on the basis of some criteria of value. A choice is then made that is perceived as the best fit to the situation. This may not be the right decision, per se, but it is the best decision in light of all the available elements considered. Therefore, if you can shape B's evaluation of the elements in the situation which might influence his or her decision, then you can create a situation in which B makes the decision you want.

Figure 4.2
Margaret and the Bank Information System

X = A wants a new info system.
X' = A needs a promotion.

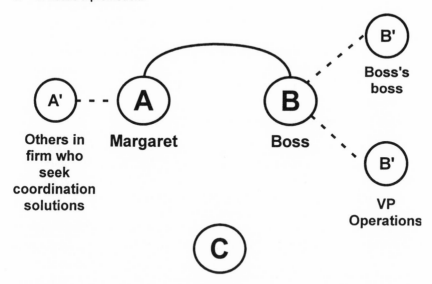

Organization Context = Bank is going through changes because of acquisitions; new system affects number of employees.

Another way in which Margaret could have solved the problem would have been to work with the other A primes, or in this case, the satellite banks. Say they are nervous, having just been taken over by the "Big Brother" bank, and are anxious about what will be coming down the pipeline. Margaret could have suggested to the managers at her level in the other banks that they might want to think about developing a means to standardize their information-system procedures. A task force among lateral peers could have been established to discuss this issue. At this meeting, Margaret could have pulled out her plan, or at least the beginnings of it. She would have been viewed as a heroine if she had.

By solving the problem in this way, you see that Margaret would have accomplished her primary goals of gaining respect, credibility, and visibility for future advancement. The A primes, the satellite banks, would have clamored for Margaret's proposal, and her boss might have responded with an emphatic "Yes!"

What other choices did Margaret have in the situation? She could have changed her desires. Remember, her desires are socially constructed based on the context. She thinks she wants respect and visibility, and maybe she truly does. But often the easiest way to change a dependency relationship is simply to alter your desires. She could have put her desires on hold. She could have even found another bank that would have drooled at her ability to develop a standardized plan. Such a bank might have seen her talents as a vital resource and would have appreciated them more. As a final note, we must add that Margaret's plan was eventually implemented. However, it was after Margaret had left the bank in frustration, spurred by her inability to effectively manage her idea and her relationships.

DOING A BEHAVIORAL ANALYSIS

Clearly, it was the wrong strategy for Margaret to escalate the conflict to the vice presidential level. Here we describe a tool, the behavioral analysis guide. It is a method for managing the problem of gaining support in lateral relationships by diagramming the process of building support. A behavioral analysis starts with the goal in mind and outlines a process of working backward, rather than pushing forward to build support. It is done by the following steps:

Step One: Define the goal or outcome you want. List this goal on the right-hand side of a sheet of paper placed horizontally.

Step Two: Who and what does the goal depend upon? Ask what decisions have to be made for the goal to be realized and who must make them. List these on the left-hand side of the paper.

Step Three: Who and what does that depend upon? Again, ask who will have to do what for each decision to work out the way you want them to. Work backwards to define what will need to happen and what each stage in the process depends on.

Step Four: Repeat the question of who and what are your goals dependent upon for each stage. Diagram the specific actions you desire for each person.

Step Five: Develop the Action Plan. As you see more clearly what specific actions each step depends upon, you can plan how to affect each stage in the process.

Example of the Behavioral Analysis

If, like Margaret, you want a promotion, your final goal is simply to obtain it. List this as the goal. Working backward, we would say that, explicitly, you must complete several critical client projects, make a certain sales quota, or meet the criteria that determine who gets promoted. List these criteria on the left-hand side of the paper.

Oftentimes, people realize at this stage that they don't really know what the criteria are. If criteria are unclear, you need to find out what those explicit criteria are, both formally from a supervisor and informally from the grapevine or network. You need to ask who decides whether you are meeting the criteria. In Margaret's case, the evaluation of her immediate boss was critical. Not rocking the boat and not upsetting the vice president were also key elements.

Let's say you determine, either by foreknowledge or by seeking information, that passing muster with your immediate supervisor is the most critical criterion for passing the review and that this person's opinion is esteemed. Then you ask, What is needed to pass that review with great acclaim? This involves knowledge of both the criteria and the boss him or herself.

For step four, you may need to ask, What is critical to your boss? What are the boss's needs or dependencies? We refer here not to personal needs so much as to the dependencies of the job. Margaret's boss, for example, has been newly placed in a coordinator position involving the other satellite banks. He very much needs to demonstrate leadership and stability. The criteria for this boss would involve building trust and camaraderie, as well as having assurance that your idea won't rock the boat.

Then, by more clearly outlining who and what each action depends upon, you can develop a more distinct and clearer plan to affect or influence these various actors. In Margaret's case, her behavioral analysis would highlight the importance of her boss's subordinates as critical to enhance the boss's reputation as a good and stable leader. She could develop an action plan that would take them into consideration. She could seek their input and involvement.

In sum, a behavioral analysis should allow you to "see" your goals and, more important, to be clear about whom your goals are dependent upon. It should allow you to see and decide what levers you can affect and plan with *specific* goals and people in mind. This, we find, is the most critical and neglected part of planning action. Most people plan abstractly, being less than specific or clear about what they really want in the end and vague about the specifics that may be needed from more than one target. Although this level of specificity may seem mundane at the outset, it should lead to more effective action planning. The process is illustrated in Figure 4.3.

JIM AND THE TAX MANAGERS CASE

Let's look briefly at a case similar to that of Margaret, but handled differently—according to a carefully presented behavioral analysis. This is

Figure 4.3
The Behavioral Analysis Model: Working Backward from the Goal

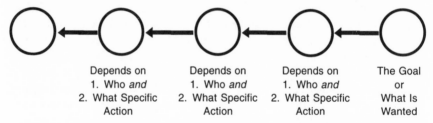

Depends on	Depends on	Depends on	The Goal
1. Who *and*	1. Who *and*	1. Who *and*	or
2. What Specific	2. What Specific	2. What Specific	What Is
Action	Action	Action	Wanted

the case of Jim, a newly hired computer analyst, and the tax managers with whom he had to interact at a large, well-known accounting firm.

Jim arrived at the accounting firm armed with all the latest information and knowledge in his field. He had recently graduated from college and had been an intern with a large accounting firm, where he was able to apply his talents of computerizing client's tax records. His internship experience had enabled him to be hired by this new firm at a premium rate. He was therefore anxious to show that he had "the right stuff" and could not only revamp their outdated, cumbersome client tax-recording system, but could also come to be viewed as a valuable resource by the firm.

The problem was that there was a lot of inertia at the accounting firm with regard to the old, outdated system. The new system—Jim's preferred system—would involve a decision to adopt new information technology and to replace existing processes. This caused considerable worry to the senior partners, who were more comfortable with the old system. "If it's not broke, why fix it?" was the attitude of the senior partners.

Using the questions posed by the behavioral analysis guide, let's analyze this situation.

Step One: Define the goal. Jim wants to have his information system implemented. He also wants recognition and respect for his efforts.

Step Two: What and whom does the goal depend upon? Before the information system is implemented, it has to be accepted as a good idea by senior partners with general consensus.

Step Three: What and whom does step 2 depend upon? In order for the senior managers to see this as a good idea, it requires some buy-in and promotion of the idea from the general managers who will be most affected by the new system on a daily basis.

Step Four: Repeat the question. What and whom does step 2 depend upon? For the managers to accept the new idea, it must meet their needs. This depends upon the managers and staff accountants perceiving that the new system is both efficient and meets the critical needs for effective interaction with clients. So here we identify one of the critical dependencies of the managers as the client relationship. All else is trivial if the client relationship is not good.

Step Five: Develop the action plan.

The necessary decisions involve (1) the acceptance of the system, (2) a decision about which information technology to use, (3) a decision to replace existing processes, and (4) a general consensus that the new system was preferable to the older, established mode. Jim might realize exactly what he needs to do and how he needs to shape his action to explicitly meet the needs of the individuals who are affected. This involves far more than an abstraction of interpersonal skills. Jim could employ his best persuasion at both the lower and upper levels. He might even be initially successful at railroading his plan through. But without the commitment and support from the lower levels—the users of the system—this success would likely be short lived.

DEVELOPING ACTION PLANS THAT ALTER POWER IMBALANCES

Performing a behavioral analysis before you act might save you from the embarrassing dilemmas in which Margaret found herself. The goal of behavioral analysis is to help you work backward to see your situation more clearly. Developing an action plan requires that you fully understand the power distribution of the organization as discussed in Chapter 2, what resources are at your disposal, as discussed in Chapter 3, and the basic principles of the ABC model from this chapter.

Emerson's second fundamental truth states that when actors are dependent, they will take action to restore the power imbalance. Power imbalances are unstable, and when we are in the dependent position, we wish very much to restore the balance of that social relationship. In other words, we work to find ways to help us achieve the goals we desire. What you are trying to accomplish—what we all want to accomplish ultimately—is to empower ourselves. No one wants to be powerless. We all want to be in control. The reason we need to assess and recognize power and dependence relationships in our lives is to determine the actions we can take that can make us more effective. To move forward with our analysis and to determine more appropriate action plans, it is necessary that we look explicitly at strategies for resolving and eliminating dependence in lateral relationships.

5

Strategic Action in the New Lateral Organization

No one wants to be powerless. We would rather be in control. Power imbalances are unstable. We strive for stability in our social relationships and in our lives. When we encounter a social situation in which we are "one-down," that is, in a dependent relationship, we wish very much to restore balance to that social relation. The actions that people take to restore balance to their social relationships has caught the attention of a variety of scholars and has resulted in the creation of influence or empowerment strategies. Countless of influence tactics, empowerment strategies, and impression-management abilities have been studied to determine their relative effectiveness in different situations.

One helpful way to look at the politics of organizations is to realize that the manifestation of what most people refer to as "politics" actually represents the actions taken by individuals to reduce their dependency in a particular social situation. If you don't want your department to be so dependent on the output of another, you may reorganize so that you won't have to be. If you want to gain more discretion over the decisions that affect your work, you may wish to neutralize your boss's power in some fashion.

TWO STRATEGIC DIRECTIONS DERIVED FROM THE ABC PARADIGM

What most people are interested in when they encounter a vexing organizational problem like Connie's, Margaret's, or Jim's is what they should do about the situation. In other words, what actions should they take? Some people think that an infinite variety of actions exists.

We experience some impatience with the typical case study approach in managing human relationships, which says, in essence, "here is a complex situation. What should Jane do?" Then, the strongest argument wins. We think there is little to be learned from such an abstract approach. In contrast, we argue that despite the infinite number of lateral relationships, the actions that are available to actors within them are relatively finite. In short, there are hundreds of potential political situations. From these, we distill a finite set of actions available for effectiveness. In this next section, we discuss the options available to an agent, A, and a target, B, in a politically determined, lateral relationship.

There are two fundamental strategic directions that A and B can take in any dependent relationship to alter the power balance. These two fundamental directions resolve to be the converse of one another, due to the reciprocal nature of the dependency relationship in the first place. One direction—the strategic course of action that applies to A—is how to eliminate his or her dependence on B, which can be accomplished in a variety of ways. The second course of action—the one that applies to B—is how to enhance his or her power in the social relationship. This too can be accomplished by a variety of tactics that may suit the situation.

STRATEGIC OPTIONS FOR A: HOW TO DIMINISH YOUR DEPENDENCE

To restore the power balance, A must find a way to diminish, and perhaps ideally, eliminate altogether, his or her dependency on B. This requires that A understand what has made him or her dependent in the first place.

To review, the sources of dependence arise under following conditions:

1. When we have a desire.
2. When we lack the ability to get what we need on our own.
3. When we lack alternatives, or we perceive that we do.
4. When others have the discretion to decide the fate of the resource we believe we need.

The tactics that you may choose directly result from these sources of dependence. This is why it is so critical that you diagnose the situations in which you are dependent in the first place.

First and foremost, you must understand that you have created your dependence and the other person's power. We give power to people. We create the power other people have over us. Conversely, you have power in a social relationship only because other people gave you that power. They give it to you because they are willing to for their own reasons, not your reasons. They are willing to desire things. They have named you as the solution to their desires.

What you can do if you are in such a situation is to extract "taxes." Therefore, if you are A, and you have allowed yourself to be dependent on B, one option available to you is to simply pay the tax. This will not diminish your dependence per se on A, but it will allow you to alter the social situation so that you can now play by the rules.

DICK AND THE TRAINING CLASS EXEMPTION

Let's look at the case of a health-related organization, where it was required that employees periodically attend certain training classes to satisfy certain criteria. In this firm, career advancement was determined according to code levels. The way codes are gained is by mastering certain experiences in the firm, but also by training.

One employee, Dick, wanted to be exempt from a certain class because he had already taken it. In fact, it was his area of study, and he was very knowledgeable in it. He thought taking this class would be a great waste of his time and talked to his boss about the situation. His boss said, "By golly, you're right, Dick. There is no point in your taking this class. We will go get an exemption." But the training supervisor did not agree. The training supervisor pulled out a piece of paper that said that all employees must take the class, and that this requirement is mandated by outside forces. Everybody agreed how silly this was, but ultimately Dick took the class and wasted his and the firm's time.

Strategic Choice 1: Paying the Tax

Dick paid the tax. One option available to Dick could have been to identify another source, a C in the context of the situation, that would have in turn put pressure on the training supervisor to exempt Dick from the course. Dick could have found someone who would have granted to him an equivalent piece of paper that he could have waved in the face of the training supervisor. But such an alternative requires time, energy, and considerable emotional investment. Sometimes it is simpler to pay the tax.

This alternative also occurs in firms where you must have a key educational credential to move forward in your career. Sometimes you simply must invest the time, energy, and resources to go and get the degree your firm is mandating you must have. Again, this strategy does not diminish your dependence—it simply forces you to play by the rules so that you are on the same playing field as everyone else.

Strategic Choice 2: Expand the Search by Finding Alternatives to Satisfy the Desire

Another strategy that is available to A is to enhance the search. Identify other B primes that might do your bidding. If you alter your belief system that says that only B can provide you with what you want, then suddenly a world of possibilities may fall upon your doorstep. As we said earlier, one of the reasons that people are in dependency situations is not because of any real structure of the world, but because of the structure they invent in their own lives. There may be many routes to solve a problem and to access a resource that you need. In the LIR admissions-decision case, Connie could have identified other schools that she wished to attend that might have given her the same quality educational experience. Very often, however, people like Connie see the situation only in terms of the number one B. Very often they are also too lazy to either think about the alternatives, or they may not wish to spend the time, money, or emotional investment establishing alternative relationships with other B primes.

This is often the case in home-care situations, where you may find yourself locked into a dependency relationship with your child's regular caretaker. On the one hand, your children have a special relationship with this person, be it a grandparent, aunt, or well-meaning friend or relative. You do not wish to disturb that relationship for a variety of reasons. However, if you find the influence this person has over your children's lives is more than you can bear, such as by allowing your children to eat chocolate or watch cartoons all day long, you may find yourself in a dilemma. The fact is, there are other B primes—such as paid professional au pairs—who do this kind of work. But perhaps you do not wish to invest the money in a professional relationship, or you do not wish to disturb the sancity of the personal relationships you share with your relative or friend. Therefore you allow yourself to stew, complain, and get an ulcer, rather than identify other B primes who could easily resolve the situation for you.

Strategic Choice 3: Coalition Building

A's third choice is to create an understanding in B that he or she has less discretion than B thinks. In truth, everyone has complete discretion. Everyone is always a free agent. But A may find ways to shape the situation so that B disbelieves his or her discretion and/or makes a free choice to see the situation your way.

We submit that in most social situations, almost all problems and conflicts resolve in a simple fashion. They are resolved by people making choices. Power is not something that is outside our organizations and our lives. Power is part of our lives. It's created through the process of our own choices. We decide for ourselves what we believe to be important, and that decision creates a structure of dependency relationships to achieve our desires. However we come to those decisions may be momentarily problematic, but always resolveable.

Coalition building is a substantial and often effective strategy for those who know how to employ this option, because it can accomplish the fundamental goal in dependent relationships: to restore the power balance. Many times, however, people in dependency relationships avoid coalition building. This results because we often become enamored with our own ideas, and our ownership of those ideas, goals, and plans prevents us from looking outside of ourselves to seek others with whom to build alliances. Coalition building is also often engaged ineffectively. Many times people seek others who have comparable "gripes" or concerns in attempting to influence targets. This is usually ineffective because these "others" are similarly powerless to affect the situation. Or, we form coalitions with others who may not represent our agendas well.

So, what does it mean to form an effective coalition? First, it is important to know what you want. This is the value of the ABC analysis. It helps to see more clearly what the agent wants, who the target is, and what other A primes or B primes may be part of the political situation. These A primes and B primes denote the potential coalition.

Let's take Dick and his situation of wanting to affect a resource from his training supervisor. We have said that in this situation, Dick is A and his training supervisor is B. Dick could have exercised the first two strategic options of (1) eliminating the dependency by getting out of this particular employment situation; or (2) paying the tax. To engage the third option of forming a coalition, Dick could have noted if there were others in an equivalant situation, such as A primes who were also dependent upon this target. If Dick could form a coalition with them, they together might represent a formidable alliance in approaching the target. By utilizing aspects of the context (the cost factor for training), Dick and the coalition may demonstrate that training these five, ten, or fifteen individuals is costly, demoralizing, and not in the target's immediate interest. Also, the coalition may have generated other alternatives for self-training.

Dick could also think about coalition building with other B-primes. This coalition would be formed as a group of supportive others who could influence the target. This is always risky but worth considering as an option when weighing advantages and disadvantages. Depending on Dick's relationship to his boss and the training supervisor's peers, there may be room for some effective coalition building on that side of the equation.

If we consider our example of Margaret, we see that her "Lone Ranger" attitude was not helpful to her in building support for her great idea of developing an information system to coordinate the banks. She might have thought about others on her side of the equation. These would be A primes—agents who may also want a better coordination system to link the banks, such as others in comparable positions at the flagship and satellite banks. She might have thought of others in the information systems department, who would potentially have much to gain from leading the bank in such a system change. In sharing her idea, she might have built sufficient social power to more effectively present this idea to the higher-ups.

Margaret also could have built a coalition on the other side of the equation: the B side. That is, she could have gained support from her boss by sharing her planning with him and bringing him into the formation of the new system plan.

Coalition building is more strategic and deliberate than merely having a friend or an ally. The ABC diagram in Figure 4.1 helps to illustrate who and where this potential coalition lies. A conscious and careful plan can be designed that not only targets B, but effectively builds a coalition that can help in achieving the goal.

Strategic Choice 4: Altering Your Desires

This leads to the fourth and last alternative: You always have the option of changing your desires which created your dependency in the first place. A can alter his or her desires. Notice that we are not saying abandon your desires, but rather alter them. In a love relationship, the agent is convinced that only one person (or in our lingo, "target") can fulfill needs and desires, and this shapes the attempt to satisfy these desires in a determined direction. As we have said, the agent can pay the tax by doing what is required: Search for others who can fulfill the desire; build a coalition to attempt to influence the target (arguably not a great option in this case); or alter the desire. The agent can decide not to love or be in love at all. Just as Dick can decide to change his desire from promotion, which brings with it certain requirements, to being satisfied with his current level in the firm.

This option of altering the desire has another side. An agent can always (and we think *should* always) ask what he or she wants and what he or she needs in any situation. In the case of the lover, the desire is a love relationship with one particular target: the need may be to be loved and to feel good about oneself. In Dick's case, he wants a promotion; he needs a secure and satisfying job. In both these cases, the need can be satisfied with a greater variety of options than either agent has yet determined. The lover can find other options to make him or herself feel better; Dick probably has more career and employment options than he has defined.

In the case of Margaret, she has defined her goal as implementing a new information system at the bank. She became, as many of us do, very attached to her plan and the implementation of it with a particular timeliness and in a particular context. However, what Margaret may have needed was a sense of esteem and recognition resulting from having a good idea recognized. She may have needed a career escalation, and she certainly needed her reputation to remain intact.

Consider how different the dependency relationship would be had Margaret redefined the goal. Two things could have happened. The first is that the options for managing the situation expand; the second is that Margaret's dependency upon one particular target diminishes. Both lead to a heightened sense of power and a sharper set of actions. In this case, if Margaret had redefined X as reputation and career escalation, Margaret would have been well advised to bring her boss into the planning stages and to take a longer time in planning the presentation and implementation of her system with these needs in mind.

Conversely, if she had redefined her desire as a need for esteem and accomplishment, a need to exhibit her real merit and brilliance, she might have reconfigured the entire situation dramatically. Rather than maintain dependency upon her boss, she could have considered an option of creating her own independent consulting firm for information systems in financial institutions under this reconfiguration. While the set of possibilities for Margaret to expand her options were varied, the important point is that an agent can always redefine the X, or goal, as a strategic option.

ANNIE AND THE GOLF OUTING CASE

In one case, a young woman who we will call Annie worked for a very prestigious law firm as a summer intern. Summer interns basically spend the summer in many law firms, operating within a "check me over" type of interaction which firms use to determine which interns might make a good future fit with the firm. It was the practice of this firm to take their summer interns out on a golf outing. Unfortunately, this created a problem. Several of the interns were women, but the golf course at the country club where the partners (all men) played forbade women to be on the greens.

Annie decided she wanted to go on this golf outing. The golf outing, by the way, was a nontrivial event, because the whole purpose of such outings is to allow the firm to size the interns up for future job possibilities. Annie felt that her nonparticipation in the golf outing would allow others to gain an unfair advantage in the competitive marketplace of the firm. So Annie went to her hiring sponsor, who said, "Well, I see your point, and yes, this is a terrible situation, but you are making a big deal out of this and it's not such a big deal. It's just one golf game, so lighten up." Annie then talked to some of the senior women in the firm, and asked what they thought of this situation. Some of them said, "Yes, its outrageous, its terrible, but why are you making such a big deal out of it?"

Annie then reevaluated her original desire to work for this prestigious law firm, as it seemed her questions were getting her nowhere. She realized if this was the kind of response she was getting both from the women as well as the men, this was not a place where she wanted to make her future law career.

Altering your desires is a very powerful mechanism. It allows you to be in control of your life and to make your own choices, so to speak.

Strategic Option 5: Affect the Context

There is one final strategic option available to A. The agent can explore the context that mitigates the power relationship between A and B. Remember, the context involves such things as

Norms

Regulation

Rules

Culture

Strategies

Policies

Often, an agent can determine that certain levers exist in the context which an agent can draw upon. For example, certain rules, or loopholes to them, may exist that Dick is unaware of about the training requirements. Certain precedents may have been established that would permit him to substitute classes with on-the-job training, or the policy may provide more time to complete the requirements.

In the case of Annie, had she decided that the firm was the one she wanted and the goal of playing golf was important, she may have uncovered some regulation or policy to pressure the target toward her goal. For example, she may have drawn upon the resources of some external regulatory group or an internal group suggesting that more females be promoted within the law firm. Margaret might have brought some governmental or competitive pressure to bear in order to heighten an argument that the firm would need to streamline operations. For Connie, her goal of gaining admission may have included finding information about the numbers of females recruited and admitted into this prestigious program. If that number had been very low, she may have brought her knowledge of this data to bear as part of her strategy for gaining admission.

Another way of utilizing the context is to consider cultural norms or beliefs that are taken for granted to draw upon. "Since we have been discussing efficiency and have been instructed to find new means of streamlining operations, I have worked out this information system." Sometimes, if a firm has adopted a new cultural paradigm or strategy such as a Total Quality Management paradigm, an agent may reference the committed belief in employee empowerment, streamlining processes, or attention to customers as a focus to use in boosting one's new idea. For example, "After benchmarking with XYZ bank, we found that our efficiency was far below theirs. We believe that has everything to do with the redundancies in our paperwork which this new information system would fix." In this way, Margaret would be referencing an aspect of the context—a belief and, more important, a commitment to a strategy already espoused by her higher-ups.

However, when the context is referenced, the important thing is to realize that aspects of the context, which are very much part of what mitigates the power balance between A and B in the first place, are very critical to consider. The question for A to ask is, What aspects of the context may be relevant to affecting B? And, like other options available to an agent, looking for a lever in the context and using it successfully is an art and must be considered within the general strategic framework.

Summary of Options for A

In sum, the options for A include

- Paying the tax.
- Expanding the search to include other options (or other Bs).
- Coalition building.
- Changing the desire (redefining X to consider need versus want).
- Affecting the context.

Often, one of the most effective actions for an agent to take is a combination of these five general strategies presented here. If Margaret had thought about the context of the bank, she might have realized that her timing was a bit problematic. She may have altered her desire from implementing the new system to getting what she really wanted, which was to enhance her reputation. Thus, including her boss might have been a good strategic choice. Finally, she could have readily built a coalition with either her boss or quite possibly some other information system people who could benefit from the system as well. She may have then been willing to pay a certain tax, and develop the plan along lines more beneficial to her boss's requirements in achieving effectiveness.

STRATEGIC OPTIONS FOR B:
HOW TO ENHANCE YOUR POWER

From B's perspective, it is very important to control the other's dependence. This may require manipulation of the situation so that you can make the person think they depend on you.

Manipulation is a word that many people rebel against. But it is part of life, and many of us are quite artful at it. When you write a resume, for example, you are manipulating another's perceptions of who you are. You convince the rest of us that you have outstanding, fantastic, and wonderful capabilities, and you use all kinds of evidencing procedures to convince the reader of your abilities. When you plan the words you will use and arrange those words in space on the paper, you are forming your words with the idea that you are going to have an effect on someone. You are working from a theory of effect. Manipulation means that you create events—that you shape events in your favor. This is what politics is all about.

It is hard to be political and to take political action unless you understand manipulation. It is difficult to be influential unless you manipulate the situation in some way or form. If you are squeamish about manipulation, then you will be squeamish about politics. You must realize that all of your actions are manipulations of one kind or another. When you seek to accomplish a particular goal, every time you act, you are in fact manipulating your environment. Though manipulation has been given a bad rap, the word comes from the same root word as management: *maun*, which means to manipulate or work upon as in cultivate. The word "management" derives from the root word, to will (*Webster's Third International Dictionary*, Unabridged).

With this in mind, realize that much of what B must do is to manipulate (or cultivate) A to believe that he or she can control his or her dependence. This means that you must shape A's perceptions of their dependence on you for the resource that you hold that A needs. One way in which this is done is to use slack resources to make others dependent on you.

Tactic 1: Controlling Resources

This first tactic to manipulate A's dependence is through control of resources, either critical and scarce resources or slack resources. Slack resources are resources or capabilities for which their owner has no need and hence are available for giving to others. We all have slack reources. For new managers the most important ones are time and energy. You should be aware of your discretionary resources that you compeltely control—your own personal slack. Time, energy, and smarts might all be put into service in solving some of the problems of the party from whom you want cooperation; alternatively, social resources such as friendship, charm, and ability contribute to others' sense of self-worth. In organizations, especially firms that are technically oriented, you can see how this tactic is used all the time.

The Case of the Technical Organization and Slack Resources

A technically oriented firm was known for its innovative products and was the standard setter for all other firms within its industry. The firm accomplished its goals as the number-one producer by hiring the most creative and intelligent engineers. These engineers designed the best products. The trouble was that every once in awhile an engineer would come up with a really great design for a new product that would rival or directly compete with one of the firm's current hot sellers. The engineer and the firm were faced with a dilemma: Should the engineer take the idea to the firm and allow them to produce the idea in house, or should the engineer find a venture capital firm that could fund her innovation from the outside?

Both choices had pros and cons from the engineer's perspective. On the one hand, keeping the concept in house meant that the engineer would sacrifice considerable potential profits but would not have the hassle and the risk of getting involved with a new startup firm. On the other hand, going outside meant that there were great profits to be made, but with considerable risk. After all, less than fifty percent of new businesses are successful after the first year.

The firm resolved this periodic problem in a nifty way. A budget was created out of excess funds to support product innovations. The firm's policy was changed to encourage, not discourage, anyone who had an innovative or rival product idea. The engineer with the idea would go to management, who would then assess the feasibility of the new product. If given the go-ahead, the engineer would develop the product in house, with all the resources of the firm at his or her disposal. The firm would give the engineer a royalty based on the ultimate long-term profitability of the new product in the marketplace.

The concept of using slack resources to create dependencies also applies to interpersonal transactions. If a manager is lucky enough to have a large budget, especially if the budget is in near liquid form where it can be pushed around, then you can allocate money to people.

You can listen to your peer tell you a story about how he can't get his boss to give him the money for this really hot idea, and you can give him the money. You can reward an employee for a brilliant idea. You can provide opportunities for people who can't get them elsewhere. The upshot is that now they are dependent on you. This is the concept of slack resources in action.

Slack resources can be anything. Time and energy, as stated earlier, is an important resource that often is overlooked. One of the ways in which people in organizations get themselves promoted is by working overtime. They do their boss's work such that their boss becomes dependent on them. When the time comes to nominate someone for an upper-level position, the boss says, "Boy, do I have someone for you. I never have seen anyone work so hard in my life. John is just the person we need around here."

Just as vital, a target can manipulate dependency by controlling critical resources. Consider the case of Francine, a new hire. When Francine is hired, her mentor assures her that a corner office will be hers. When Francine arrives on her first day, the office manager who controls these resources (and is incidentally miffed that Francine's mentor went over her head) tells Francine that offices are very scarce, and only those who have been in the firm for five to ten years receive corner offices. Francine quickly learns, too, that this office manager tightly controls everything, even file cabinets and the work order to obtain them. Completely unaware of the office manager's presence during interviews, Francine now realizes her newfound dependence on this woman, whose ability to control resources is her sole source of power.

Tactic 2: Shaping Other's Perceptions

This leads to a second, but related tactic derived from the ABC paradigm. B can control A's perception of his or her contributions and abilities in a situation, or can control the perception of A's value and importance as a supplier to others. This involves shaping other's perceptions of how important you are to them.

The Case of the Frustrated Telephone Company Worker

Mary, a telephone company worker, had been hired by a larger telecommunications firm with the promise that she would be assigned a higher level of responsibility than what she had experienced previously at a smaller telecommunications firm. But what Mary did not know was that she was signing on at this firm during a time of great change. The CEO had been replaced, and the new CEO was preaching integrative, team-oriented management. This would have required that the company restructure itself in a way that did not suit Mary's original goals.

As these things go, during a time of great change, there are likely to be not one but multiple reorganizations. When the first reorganization occurred, Mary bit her lip and stayed low. She focused on the new work she had been assigned. When the second reorganization threatened, Mary requested a meeting with the supervising vice president, who was in charge of the reorganization. She made it clear that the Los Angeles market, for which she had been originally responsible, represented almost half of the total capital budget, amounting to over one billion dollars of spending. She suggested to the vice president that this market required special attention, and as such, should be split apart from the other markets the company served.

Simultaneously, a crisis occurred in the Los Angeles market that caught the attention of the division president. Why was this not forseen, the company president asked? Mary stepped in quickly and resolved the crisis. In the third reorganization, Mary was named as the head of the specialized Los Angeles market and was heralded for her heroism and quick thinking in solving company blunders.

Tactic 3: Eliminating the Competition

A third tactic is to eliminate the competition for your resources or your capabilities. This tactic often is very manipulative, and people sometimes rebel against it because they see that this is direct manipulation.

The Faculty Tenure Case

Take the case of two professors, both of whom were from the same department, hired in the same year, and who were up for tenure at the same time. The university only had one position for tenure available. Only one of the faculty candidates would get the position.

Both faculty members were good. They had done adequate research and had letters from colleagues saying how esteemed their research was. They both produced strong teaching evaluations showing how students respected their teaching abilities and learned volumes from them. Both had adequately served their university on departmental committees and professional associations.

But one of the faculty members had been recently divorced. And he had been seen frequently with one of the female graduate students. The other faculty member, a female who was the sole breadwinner for her family, simply stated in passing one day to her department chair how often she had noted that the graduate student was with the other nontenured faculty member on campus. She did not state that the two must be involved. She simply stated the facts that these two individuals had been seen together.

Because it was the university's policy to frown upon sexual liaisons between faculty and students, especially for sexual harassment reasons, the male, divorced, nontenured faculty member was called into the department chair's office and asked if anything was going on. He denied the charge. Probably nothing was. But it was no surprise to all when the woman received tenure, and the man did not.

Tactic 4: B Can Expand the Numbers of A Primes

In this tactic, B can work to be sure he or she has alternatives to the agent and thus reduce his potential dependency. That is what firms are doing when they keep a thick file of applications on file and what many firms do when they actually hire slack resources. The Big Five firms, for example, are in an almost constant state of recruitment. This is done in part to manage growth and in part to manage the cyclical nature of their business. They operate with an understanding of a fountain system. People come in, move up, and are quite often retained by firms. These firms keep up a steady supply of new recruits and are spared getting into an overly dependent situation or labor crunch.

Most businesses operate this way. It sometimes baffles young students in university towns. "We are learning so much about management, why do we have so many poor bosses in town who don't seem to care much about how they treat their employees?" While these reasons may be the subject of philosophical debate, one reason to be sure is that colleges provide a more constant supply of workers, willing to work for minimum wage, which results in a diminished dependency upon the workers.

Tactic 5: Forming Coalitions

A final tactic is to form coalitions with others who have power over your target. Coalition building is what organizations are all about. You see this clearly when you are trying to get a promotion. A group of people size you up to see if you have what it takes to make it as a member of their club. Organizations form coalitions around the important decisions. This is why so many organizational decisions—the decisions around which power organizes—are decided in group meetings.

The Case of the Feminist Arts Festival

A well-known nationwide arts festival created by and for women received an application from one woman who sculpted naked women.

She was a radical lesbian who had a personal rule that no man should ever look upon her scupltures. She stated such on her application form for the arts festival, but apparently the organizers of the festival did not pay attention to her rule. A problem occurred when two men who attended the festival attempted to look at her artwork; she became offended and punched them out. This created a major crisis for the organization, right in the middle of the festival. The woman maintained that she had written her policy on her application form and had been allowed admission to the festival accordingly. The head honchos of the organization maintained that the festival was for everyone—if she had such a policy on her application, they did not see it, and anyway, she should have known better.

The craftswomen were very concerned about the issues. Eventually they solved the problem themselves by recognizing the limits of authority. Since they couldn't control the chief honchos without they themselves getting thrown out of the festival, even though they sympathized with the woman's plight, they organized volunteer female guards who would station themselves around the woman's booth. If a man approached, they simply locked arms and charmed the man away. They formed a coalition to divert the man's attention. The craftswomen constructed a situation using the capabilities they had so they could respect the lesbian craftwoman's wishes.

Strategic Option 6: B Can Affect the Context of a Situation

Just as the agent can draw upon elements of the context, in the form of rules, regulations, norms, and strategic commitments, so can B elicit elements of the context to further solidify A's perception of dependency. Imagine a situation in which an agent seeks a promotion from B. "Steve, we'd like to promote you, but you know we can't because corporate is after us to hire a woman. Well, just keep up the good work. Corporate tells us next year might look better for you."

Or, if Dick's boss wanted to enhance Dick's dependency, he might say something like, "Well Dick, if you aren't willing to go through the training, we've been told to increase our recruiting effort this year; these new recruits will most likely be better trained." In both cases, the target is drawing on elements of the organizational context to enhance A's perception of dependency.

Frequently, B is better informed than A about the firm's context. This makes it particularly easy for B to draw on elements of the context. Consider the meeting in which A's proposal gets sidelined by B with this familiar phrase: "Well, that's a nice idea, but we tried that very thing a few years ago and it didn't work at all." It could well be that the idea and what was tried and why it didn't work were an entirely different situation. Nevertheless, B's knowledge of the context can be drawn on to effectively close out A's argument, unless A is smart and recognizes the manipulation.

Ben, the Newly Hired Accountant

Consider the situation in which Ben is a young hire in an accounting firm. He has requested more home-office-based assignments and to travel a bit less. "Well, Ben, I really need you on my team," retorts his boss. "You know, I will be performing your six month employment appraisal and your promotion is entirely up to me. You may not know this, so let me fill you in—willingness to travel is the most important criteria for retention here." In this rather unpleasant manipulation, Ben's boss has drawn on a norm and a specific criteria of which Ben is unaware. It doesn't even happen to be true, in this case, but the boss as the target has certainly enhanced Ben's sense of dependency. Ben's recourse is to be smart and to find out if this contextual information is true. If so, he can weigh his options accordingly. If not, he can attempt to educate his boss about the alternatives available.

Managing lateral relationships and understanding the distribution of power that provides their context is the resolution of all these individual choices. When you get ticked off at someone—when you can't understand why you can't get things done—it all can be traced back to a simple ABC analysis of this fundamental relation. Power distributes itself through this social system depending on how all the individuals take these choices. It's not a mystery, it's not something that comes from outside, it's not something that you buy—it's something that is created through the process of social exchange.

Political action can be defined quite simply as the actions people take to restore the power imbalance. The political tactics that can be used in these situations are derived directly from the ABC paradigm. The value of the ABC paradigm is that once you analyze a situation according to the model, you can then utilize your knowledge to influence the levers of the situation to suit your own interests. Our lives are about the choices we make. The more effectively we can assess whether the value of the goals that are to be achieved are worth investing in in the first place, the more likely we are to utilize our freedom of choice to make the right choices, rather than merely accepting our powerlessness.

6

Action Plans in the New Lateral Organization

In this chapter we will consider how to plan political action. We will examine tactics for confronting and managing the vexing organizational problems you may be trying to solve.

The ABC paradigm is helpful in diagramming lateral networks and identifying some natural courses of action that can be taken in a given situation. It is a useful organizing device to help you identify what political actions might be considered based on the resources you may hold. And, it identifies the players, both the obvious and often the not so apparent. By making the targets, potential targets, agents, and potential coalitions more transparent, planning action becomes a more deliberate activity. And so it should be. Some people deliberate more carefully about what shoes to buy or which car to drive than they would about actions that have an impact on their careers—and in some cases, the success or failure of those careers. This chapter is about planning political action that is designed to preclude the hapahazard strategies many of us use in politically charged situations.

Assume you know what you want. Having stated or articulated to yourself what you want, you also have specified those parties upon whom you are going to be dependent. You have constructed a political relationship for yourself. In political action the details are very important. Very often outcomes are won or lost on the basis of the tiniest details.

In order to plan political action, you must be in command of the particulars of the situation, the actors involved, and the ways by which the outcomes of the situation may be generated. You must also be aware of your strategic options. Finally, you must be aware of the limits of your ability to implement any political tactic and their costs and consequences.

Successful and smart political action requires that you become aware of all the details of the situations in which you have allowed yourself to be dependent. This means that you will need to analyze, in great and considerable detail, the ABCs of the situations you are trying to confront so that you know where you stand. In other words, you are a central part of the lateral network that is constructed in part by organizational realities and in large part by what you really want. Then you can make a choice to accept your dependence or empower yourself. In either case the choice will be yours.

MAPPING THE BRENDA AND WENTON CASE

With a basic understanding of the ABC framework and the choices for strategic action, let's apply this analysis to three cases of vexing organizational problems. The first is the case of Brenda and Wenton.

Wenton arrived at his office one day and was met with a surprise request from his boss. He was told that he would have the responsibility to oversee the departure of Brenda, a clerk and computer analyst who had decided to leave the firm for greener pastures elsewhere.

Brenda worked for the planning department along with Wenton, and her job had been to maintain the computer files on all financial and nonfinancial indicators used in scheduling the plant's activities. Although her status was that of a clerical employee, Brenda worked on critical information that was central to the functioning of the plants for which Wenton was responsible.

Later that morning, Wenton stopped by Brenda's desk to ask about the files. Brenda gestured to a heap of diskettes, collected papers, computer printouts, and other assorted data piled sporadically across her desk. Wenton asked whether Brenda had a file library by which the collections of material could be organized. Brenda looked confused and responded that she never had time for something like that.

Over the next three days, Wenton kept trying to get Brenda's attention. He could not make sense of the jumble of folders and diskettes on her desk without her help. Each time Wenton requested help from Brenda, she reported that she was busy getting out last minute reports before she fled. Meanwhile, Wenton's boss asked how the transition was going. "That Brenda," said Wenton's boss, "she really is something. Such an efficient worker. I'm sorry we have to lose her."

So was Wenton. In the middle of the second week prior to Brenda's departure, he woke up in the middle of the night in a cold sweat. In two weeks time, Brenda was leaving and he didn't have a clue about what he could do to get her to cooperate.

To analyze this case, we must first identify the players. The first question to ask is, Why is Wenton having difficulty gaining Brenda's cooperation? What is the root cause of Wenton's powerlessness to take action?

Wenton, as actor A, is dependent on Brenda, actor B, for a resource: the knowledge Brenda has concerning her files. In effect, the master file, or the X, does exist. It simply exists within Brenda's brain. Wenton's dilemma is that he must access it.

Why has Wenton granted Brenda the power of this social relationship? Because he desires something. He may desire to please his boss. He may want to impress his boss so that he can be considered for a raise. He may simply not want to screw up his relationship with his boss. Now if Wenton was leaving the firm along with Brenda, he may not give a flying fig whether or not he is able to access Brenda's knowledge.

This in fact, is Brenda's situation. She has discretion over how she chooses to spend her time during her last days. She could spend them with Wenton helping him out or she could go out with the girls for long coffee breaks.

Wenton has allowed himself to be dependent also because he views her as the only person who has access to the information he seeks. But the truth is that Brenda is not the only person with this information. Others with whom she interacted on a daily basis held the same information, albeit piecemeal. But Wenton was not willing to ferret out the information from a variety of sources. He framed and reinforced the situation in such a way that he was solely dependent on Brenda.

C also factored strongly in this case, in that the context exerted a powerful influence over Wenton's behavior. The norms of the firm were such that if you were assigned a problem, you should handle it on your own. Escalating problems to higher-ups was discouraged. The potency of this norm regulated Wenton's behavior, at least until the day before Brenda was scheduled to leave. Wenton then explained to his boss that for a variety of reasons, there had not been sufficient time to resolve the situation. This did not sit well with his boss, who reminded Wenton that he was being ineffective and needed to be in better control of his employees, a fact that rendered Wenton all the more insecure. At the eleventh hour, Wenton's boss then took charge and struck a deal with Brenda to remain an extra week at higher pay to finalize the file review.

The ABCs of Lateral Networks

Using Figure 6.1, we can now see what options are available to the various actors, how the context influences actions, and the essential power relationship between Brenda and Wenton.

Figure 6.1
Brenda and Wenton

X = Wants the operating files.
X' = Wants the boss to believe he is competent.

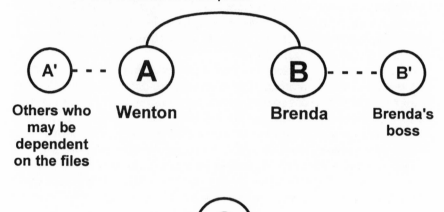

Organizational Context = A culture of managing problems at the lowest level without the supervisor's involvement.
Timing issue: Brenda is leaving.

What options were available to Wenton as A? First, he could alter his desires. He could tell himself that it does not matter whether or not Brenda gives him the information he seeks because he never really wants to get promoted in the firm anyway.

He also could pay the tax by finding out what Brenda wants and paying the price. Maybe what Brenda wants is to socialize during her last days. He could accommodate her interests and still negotiate a time frame for getting his goal accomplished. Perhaps he could take her out for a drink after work and spend the evening going over her files.

He could identify alternatives by finding out who else in the firm has the knowledge he seeks. He may have to get it piecemeal from others, but it can be done.

He also could attempt to shape Brenda's discretion in her decision making about how she spends her time during her remaining days. There are a variety of ways in which this could be accomplished. This requires looking at the situation from B's perspective to identify what externally controlled factors might allow Brenda to make a choice about how she spends her time in a way that favors Wenton's best interests.

He just might have some slack resources available that Brenda might appreciate. He could, for example, utilize his own time. He could promise Brenda he will work overtime to complete his work and her remaining work if she would simply sit down with him and help him organize her files.

He also could eliminate the competition for her attention. He could make certain that the others, the A primes, who are competing for Brenda's attention do not exist. He could tell them that he must work alone with Brenda and see if it flies. Or he could invent an immediate crisis for the other A primes that they must work on, which would distract them from Brenda.

How could Wenton make the context work for him? He might remind Brenda that he will be writing her future letters of reference. Since Brenda is leaving for greener pastures, she isn't currently dependent on Wenton, but he may gain some leverage by reminding Brenda that she may need him in the future. Or, he could find a way to make her dependent on him for something he has that she needs right now. He could also remind her that he has helped her on a variety of other projects. Or he could form a coalition such that Brenda's only choice is to help him out with his problem.

Each of these tactics are bound to be met with varying degrees of success. What could Wenton have done in this situation that might have been more politically effective? If we were to build a causal model or behavioral analysis as we outlined in Chapter 5 of what Wenton needs to accomplish in this situation, it would begin with the word *knowledge*.

In a causal model, we begin with the goal and work backwards. What is necessary for Wenton to have in place so that he can gain the knowledge from Brenda that he seeks? He must find a way for Brenda to spend *time* with him. And so,

$$knowledge = time$$

How can he get her to spend time with him? It seems that there is a lot of competition for her time from others who need information from her before she leaves. Therefore he must find a way to manage his *competition*.

$$knowledge = time - competition$$

Therefore, any one of the competition alternatives is likely to be successful. But there is another piece to the puzzle that must fall into place before the situation can resolve itself. Brenda must *agree* that his competition is nonexistent; or better yet, that among the B primes with whom Brenda could be spending her time, Wenton is the one she will choose.

$$knowledge = time - competition + agreement$$

A Behavioral or Causal Model of Action

What is Wenton's goal?	To obtain Brenda's knowledge about operating systems.
Who or what does that depend upon?	Brenda.
Who or what does that depend upon?	Brenda must agree to spend time.
Who or what does that depend upon?	Brenda must be persuaded to spend time with Wenton or Brenda must have less competition for her time.
Who or what does that depend upon?	Competition must be reduced or coopted to assist Wenton in obtaining Brenda's time.
Who or what does that depend upon?	Wenton must determine what resources he holds to obtain cooperation from other employees and from Brenda.

The Behavioral or Causal Model Analysis

The causal model is a tool. To figure out what Wenton should do, we begin with his goal first, and work backward. By repeatedly asking who or what does each action depend upon, we come up with levers Wenton can push and actions he can take. The bottom line is if Wenton is able to identify exactly what resources Brenda needs from him, he can alter the power imbalance such that it is in his favor. In Wenton's case, he could have asked himself what resources he had that Brenda might need from him. One resource he held that he did not take advantage of was Brenda's reputation. She would not have appreciated it if he had bad-mouthed her to others in the firm just before her final departure; she wanted to leave with smiles and glory. And, as the ABC analysis and the causal model highlight, Wenton had other resources in the firm in the form of other employees—his own lateral network—who could help him to influence Brenda. Wenton failed to see that mutual dependencies existed in the situation, so he was unable to resolve his dilemma in any way other than to go to his boss. His chosen course of action only had the outcome of making himself look bumbling and ineffective.

THE COMPUTER SKILL CASE

Consider the case of the lowly staff analyst, Rick, who was promoted through the ranks to serve as a staff assistant to a group of operational auditors at Blue Cross/Blue Shield. Rick was pleased with his promotion except for one problem—he had a burning desire to become an investment portfolio manager. The problem was that auditing and finance were considered wholly different operations, and transfers between areas were never considered. His boss did not support the change. No wonder—Rick lacked the necessary education and had no experience as a financial analyst. Therefore his chances of moving into this other area at his firm were quite slim.

To solve the problem, let's answer the questions suggested by the behavioral or causal model. On whom is Rick dependent? What is the source of his dependence? Who are the actors in the situation? What resources does he have that they might need?

Rick, actor A, is dependent on his boss, the B in this situation, to allow him an opportunity to make the career change, the X. He is dependent strictly because this is something he desires. However he does not have support at the moment to do so because he does not have the qualifications. The C, the context and norms that allow for movement across areas, is holding Rick back. His boss thinks highly of his job performance in his current job, but C is in the way.

Let's build a causal model:

1. Rick wishes to get promoted to a financial management area. He wants to make a career change, ideally to investment management.

2. To achieve that goal, there must first be an opportunity in the area where he hopes for a career. Therefore, for him to get anywhere, he needs an opportunity. It turns out at this firm there was no in-house investment function. Although considerable financial analysis work went on, investment counseling was outsourced.

3. In his current firm, given the way the firm operates, he needs either educational credentials or to have demonstrated mastery through experience. Currently he has neither. Therefore he needs qualifications.

4. If he had qualifications, he could be doing investment-management activities elsewhere. The rub of the problem is that he wants to do it in his current firm, ideally without paying the tax of going back to school part time at night. So there is an intermediate step that is required here; he needs support from the higher-ups at his firm to give him the chance he needs to move into this other area.

The causal model then can be stated as follows:

$$\text{career change} = \text{opportunity} + \text{support} + \text{qualifications}$$

Analysis of the Behavioral Model and Alternatives

What are the possible alternatives available to Rick in this situation? First and foremost, he can alter his desire. He can say, "Well, it was a nice idea, and I really would have liked investment portfolio management, but I just wasn't cut out for it, and this is life."

Also, he can pay the tax. He can go back to school and get the educational credential necessary to accomplish his goals.

He can also find other alternatives. This offers a host of possibilities. He could find an alternative mentor who might sponsor his arrival into the investment area. However, what is the likelihood that another mentor might do this for him if the C of the firm says not to? This would entail a political risk that the mentor would have to take and it is unlikely that the mentor would favor Rick's interest over his own. He could find other firms that may accept his current qualifications and hire him into a money-management position simply by virtue of his desire. This takes time and effort, however, and few firms offer the level of prestige he has at his current firm.

The trouble here is that Rick has little to offer the organization. There is nothing in particular that the firm is dependent on him for. Therefore there are few, if any, levers he can pull in the situation to accomplish his desires. This is the central problem that must be resolved.

It just so happened that this was 1982, and personal computers or PCs were just being introduced to companies across the nation. Rick took the initiative to learn how to use the only personal computer in his department. He became the departmental expert. His expertise on a scarce but vital commodity landed him a promotion in the budget department. He didn't take the job because he wanted it. It was a lousy job. But, it did allow Rick to use his newfound computer skills to work on the company budgets. He took the job because it was in the finance division and thus offered a pathway to his chosen career.

Rick successfully computerized the corporate budget on a PC. This caught the attention of the controller and the VP of finance, mostly because they were computer illiterate and needed Rick to explain to them how they could access the monies in their own budgets. Rick became a central figure to ask questions and give guidance for using the PC for financial applications.

Soon others became dependent on him for his PC knowledge. Rick now had available a resource—PC skills—that others in the firm required. He used his visibility to ask for an opportunity in in-house investment management. He was told that such a function did not formally exist, but there had been discussion of formalizing an in-house investment function.

So Rick hit an obstacle—no opportunities. Meanwhile, still believing he was destined for a money-management career, Rick completed his undergraduate degree at night. He paid the tax. With the permission of his boss, the VP of finance allowed him to conduct, on his own, a feasibility study on in-house investment management. He wisely spent a lot of his time on the investment study, and the critical tasks in his budgeting work fell by the wayside. This allowed him to persuade the VP of finance to pull him from his budget work and to replace him so that he could continue his feasibility study.

His study yielded the following information: The financial operations of the company had begun to deteriorate, and in 1985, investment income was the only thing that was keeping the firm profitable. The corporation began to utilize debt to finance some of its large capital projects rather than reduce the corporate liquidity further. Rick noted that the firm had no in-house experience in this. Rick then suggested to the VP that they needed a banker who could offer a proposal. The choice of bankers then became a political football, where the board of directors largely relied on Rick's investment-study findings. Eventually Rick was asked to head up a full-liability, money-management group to handle the problem.

By following the simplified causal model, you can see how pieces of this picture fell into place for Rick. First, he made the firm dependent on his special skills. Second, he created an opportunity for investment-analysis work when one did not exist. Simultaneously, he paid the tax to get one of the educational credentials required. This combination of events allowed him to gain support for his career change. Rick turned the dependency situation around—the firm became dependent upon him and began offering him various kudos to persuade him to stay with them. He is now happily ensconced in a financial-investment area in a different firm, where he has already been promoted twice.

We can see how this situation could have easily gone awry and followed its "natural course." Rick was in a frustrating career situation, of the variety that occurs every day in our world. He wanted more and knew intuitively (as many people know) that he was capable of much more, but he was held back by the norms that say, "You can't do that—we don't do that here; we don't transfer people between and among departments." All of which translates to the following: "You are stuck. But chin up, now—it could be worse." But his story has a cheerful ending. Rick was smart, and even more important, Rick was deliberate in planning his political actions. And although he paid the tax of obtaining some additional credentials, that alone didn't propel him from a staff assistant into a powerful position in this firm. Paying the tax alone wouldn't have facilitated a transfer, because in this firm (as in many firms), that "wasn't the way it was done."

So, how do you know whether it's smart to pay the tax? An important part of planning is examining the costs and the benefits of what you really want. Sometimes the cost is greater than what you thought you wanted, or what you thought you wanted has an impact or consequence that you definitely *don't* want.

ISSUES IN PLANNING POLITICAL ACTION

A major issue is the value to you of achieving the goal. Because most things are not of infinite value, it is useful ahead of time to identify how invested you are in achieving your goal. For example, ask yourself, Will you commit suicide if you do not get your peer to let you use his computer? Will your life collapse if you do not get into the school of your choice? Probably and hopefully not—but your life will require redirection. Thinking about a worst-case scenario helps here. Although these examples are extreme, the point is that goals need to be prioritized. They are not all equal and every battle needn't be won.

The Bail-Out Point

A second issue is your bail-out point. A way to think about this is to consider at what point you will end your quest for the goal—the point when you will decide to drop the issue rather than invest further in it. For example, should Connie have lied to the admissions director in order to assure herself a place in the upcoming class? How many training classes would Dick have been willing to take? Would Wenton have been willing to beg Brenda for the files or promise her what he couldn't deliver? The reason it is useful to have a point initially is that it is easy in the heat of the battle to lose sight of what you were initially after. Sometimes we obtain the goal but burn all our (carefully constructed) bridges in the process—a cost that may be greater than we initially wanted to incur.

What Do You Want?

A third issue to consider is if what you *think* you want is really *what* you want. Being sure the goal as defined is the one you really want. We get committed to goals and actions often before we really think about whether the goal is what we really want. All sorts of tendencies to "win" take over and cloud the initial goal. Social psychologists have long been fascinated with the aspect of human behavior dubbed "scarcity," or the threat of loss. Simply put, when some item or resource which we think we want becomes scarce, or we are threatened with losing it all together, its perceived value goes up. This is what happens when toy stores have a "limited" number of the number-one toy; the car you are interested in is suddenly "the last one on the lot," or its price "may go up tommorrow"; or when the recruiter learns you have two more pending job offers.

And when we are threatened with losing a resource all together, our desire for it is likely to skyrocket. We want to stay in this job all the more when it looks as though we might lose it. Suddenly, we forget the years of complaining about the position, the nuisance work, our insipid coworkers, the bad management, and lousy hours when the company embarks on a wave of layoffs and our self-esteem is threatened. For some, the word "no" is motivation enough to act, even though "yes" isn't what they really wanted.

This is why it's important to think long and hard about what you really want before you embark on political action. If you don't, you may have to pay a big price for something that isn't what you really wanted. And, the desire to win only for the sake of winning can't be the goal in itself. You may "win the battle and lose the war," if what you thought you wanted harms your chances for the larger goal.

What Do You Need?

Let's recall the case of Margaret and her efforts to gain support for a new information system. Margaret would define her goal, the X, as implementing the information system. When we step back and ask, "What did Margaret really want," the goal of getting the information system in place had a very great price for her. Another way to think about it is what did Margaret really need?

If Margaret had stopped to think about it, what she needed was a good reputation and the boss's and her coworkers' applause for her contribution. If she had defined the goal this way, she might have realized that there were many ways to enhance her reputation. When viewed from this vantage point, pushing the particular idea of the information system might begin to lose its luster. Or, she might have combined her goals into one—keeping and enhancing her reputation while moving the system forward, with her coworkers' and boss's input. The cost of "winning this battle" spurred Margaret to go over her boss's head, at a huge cost: It would cost her the goal.

What Is the Cost?

Margaret's bail-out point would have been clearer had she thought about what she really wanted. Another way to identify your bail-out point is to identify the costs associated with the political actions you are considering. When we think about costs, its helpful to think about the real, nonmonetary costs of what we want both from our own (or A's) perspective and from the target (or B's) perspective. Oftentimes, we become enamored with our own ideas and fail to realize the nontangible costs our great ideas pose to ourselves and to the target. What we think is a small cost, may have large and looming implications for the target. An office which stands empty may seem like a reasonable resource to request, but for the target, it creates the perception of inequity and may well spin off a host of requests from others who would see the allocation of space as "unfair." "Why does Tony have a larger office than mine while I have been here longer?" The simple request for a vacant office is not simple at all within this organizational context.

There are three other costs to consider. First is the overall cost of implementing the action. Is the action that you are planning within your available or easily attainable resources and capabilities? If not, then you may wish to reconsider whether the action is worth it in the first place. If you must invest a lot of energy, time, and effort to gain the resource you need to alter the power balance of the situation, then it may not be worth it.

Consider the example of the faculty member who wanted to be promoted. His colleagues did not view him as "making the grade," so they denied him his promotion. The faculty member then began to engage in a variety of political acts directed to affect his colleagues, the dean, the provost, and the president of the university. Eventually he decided to sue the university for his promotion, at great cost to himself. He didn't get it.

Another cost to consider is future relationships. Organizations are systems—systems of relationships. A disturbance in one relationship is likely to have a ripple effect upon another. The faculty member who sued ended up doing permanent harm to his reputation and long-term relationships. Because the academic community has strong networks with faculty at many universities, this ended up harming him for several years.

One former M.B.A. student tells a story about a time when he gave into the request of one unit for a software graphics order. Another competing unit also made the same request. The problem was that there was only one software package that could be allocated at that time. He gave the package to the first unit utilizing a simple coin toss. Because the first unit received the software, they were able to do great things. Their presentations were sleeker and better than those of their competing department. They received numerous accolades for the professionalism of their work. Suddenly members of the first unit were getting promoted, while the members of the other department lagged behind. Ironically, when the student was eventually moved out of his purchasing area, he ended up in the second unit's department with a cluster of angry employees all around him.

What Actions Are Legitimate?

You must also consider the legitimacy of your actions. Although it is within your abilities to take any action you please, there will be an effect upon the context resulting from your actions. Within the context are your evaluators who assess whether your action is within your province to take. Sometimes people think they are being assertive in going ahead with their plans, despite formidable resistance, only to find themselves forever tainted in the firm as someone who doesn't "play by the rules," or who is a "troublemaker."

What makes actions illegitimate? One way is if there are great costs to the other party by the magnitude of your request, or if those costs go against precedent, violating the "way things are done" in your firm. Here, we advocate that after you assess what the goal costs *you*, take some time and think about the cost of your desire from the target's perspective. Costs are not mere monetary expenses, which are usually the easiest to rationalize. We can think of costs in a few major ways beyond the monetary implications. These costs fall into three categories:

- the cost to other relationships.
- the cost of precedent.
- the cost to reputation.

The Cost to Other Relationships

Think about what your request costs the target politically, or in other words, what other important relationships might be affected within your own or the target's network. Requests take place within political context, and those contexts are formed by the numerous other relationships your boss, or the target for your request, must satisfy.

Consider the case of the relatively new employee who asked for her own office. The employee, Marie, was frustrated sharing an office, thinking it beneath her experience level and, frankly, her dignity. "I haven't had to share an office in ten years," she reasoned. "Besides, there is an office on the eighth floor about to become vacant when Joe retires, and if I don't ask for it, someone else surely will." And besides, Marie had pulled in several big accounts recently and thought the boss would be eager to demonstrate his appreciation. And so, Marie confidently approached her boss with the seemingly simple request for the coveted office. She was surprised when the boss turned down her request with little fanfare. Her surprise turned to personal frustration when the office continued to sit vacant several months later. She began to think the boss must dislike her.

"What would it have cost him to give me the office? It is such a simple thing to do," Marie complained. In fact, the office would have cost the boss a great deal. Unknown to Marie was the very simple matter of context. Others had waited for offices far longer than the three months Marie had been employed, and the boss had entertained (and turned down) four other requests in the past six months. Giving an office to Marie would have affected numerous other relationships, putting the boss in a bad light with others who would perceive favoritism. To boot, Marie's own peers may well have resented her for getting something unfairly.

A simple thing to remember is that almost all resources we desire cost someone something. Knowing what it costs and who it costs is important so that we truly understand the real magnitude of our request. By being more aware of the true costs for our target, we can better shape the request and be more effective. These costs can be understood only when looked at from the perspective of the other person's reality.

The Cost of Precedent

A second cost to consider is the cost of precedent. If what you are requesting, however small and seemingly easy for the target to deliver, goes counter to established norms, rules, a culture, or a regulation, the cost is often larger than we think. Something the firm has never done before, however useful, promising, or successful in other contexts, is likely to be very costly and risky to a target. You may have a brilliant idea, but if this firm has not tried it, the risk is high. This was the situation for Dick. His request of transferring across departments went counter to the company practices. There is a perceived fear that "changing precedent" will set off a wave of similar requests. Most likely, this anticipated wave of comparable requests never materializes, but the fear that it might creates a real cost.

The Cost of Reputation

Some things cost in terms of reputation. We may think our brilliant idea enhances a firm and even in the process advances a particular target's reputation. "Our department will save money, and the boss will love me," we think. The truth is, if you are working for me, and you've come up with an idea to improve processes, production, or something which I haven't thought about, your good idea can make me look very bad indeed. I've been here for ten years. You've been here for ten days. Worse yet, your idea is probably right. Why didn't I see that or think of it, and what will my higher-ups think of me that I didn't?

This is the cost that underlies the young turk–old turk battle. New, younger workers enter a firm. Immediately, they see many problems in process, production, antiquated management styles, and service, to name a few. Coming up with improvements seems like the obvious thing to do. If they are smart, as today's work force is, and if they've been trained to look for and analyze problems, as today's business school graduates have been, chances are they see lots of things begging for improvement. Some eager employees begin to bring ideas for change forward almost immediately. What is forgotten is that the processes, production, style, and services they want to improve were put in place by the very people they are bringing their great ideas to. And sometimes, the eager employees blame their bosses for being "stuck in the past" and unwilling to change. Another round of old turk–young turk. The point is, it is important to think about whose ideas *our* ideas change and what the cost to their reputation is for not having previously realized the need themselves.

Consider the situation of our colleague Jeff, who brought forth a new course in entrepreneurship for a business school. It's an improvement to the curriculum, in demand by students, and is state of the art, being offered at the most elite M.B.A. schools. Jeff suggests his new course should replace the antiquated management course. The old turks raise eyebrows. They didn't know their course was antiquated. Besides, old turk 1 created the course ten years ago; old turk 2 likes teaching it, and old turk 3 should have thought of offering this course because it is in his area of proported expertise. All the old turks vote no. Medium-old turk 4 votes no—his own new course got shot down last year, and he is feeling smug. Medium-old turk 5 also votes no. He doesn't want to support a precedent of changing the curriculum because he hasn't come up with a new course, ever. Medium-old turk 6 votes no because the new course might change the precedent of course sequencing and his established routine while demanding more preparation work for him as well.

Jeff's stellar new course gets voted down six to one. "What a stuffy old place," Jeff thinks. "You'd think they'd be glad I came up with a new course because it helps the school's reputation. It doesn't cost those guys anything to put my new course in place." This thinking is wrong and gets people with good ideas in trouble all the time.

In this case, the course had one large cost which prevented Jeff's success. The course costs the targets too much reputation and precedent. Reputation and precedent costs are among the highest costs to consider when planning political action. Had Jeff understood and counted the cost of his request, he could have managed the process very differently. For one, he could have modified his new course to include elements of the established course, and framed it as building on the established courses, because "they are so valuable and vital." He might have recognized the real cost of reputation and included some of the old and medium-old turks in planning the new venue.

It's important to think about the real cost to a target, if you are to succeed with planning and executing effective political action. When ideas cost targets by affecting other relationships, reputations, or precedent, these costs are nontrivial. Such costs may affect the target's own standing in the firm and his or her potential career. Sometimes they affect the target's own job or the way she or he performs that job. See how these costs go well beyond the monetary cost of the desired resource? "What's an office cost him?" asks Marie. His reputation of fairness with fifty others, say we.

BUILDING COMMITMENT TO COSTLY REQUESTS

New ideas almost always have costs, beyond the transparent monetary cost. Innovation by its nature disrupts the status quo, or it wouldn't be innovation. When your idea has costs associated with it, you need to determine what those costs are and work within that framework. We advocate that people should be successful with their ideas and plans rather than frustrated by closed doors. To do so involves thinking as much about the process of venturing a new idea as the idea itself.

One tactic of doing so is to build commitment. Comitment to the idea needs to be built, and this is costly, in time and reputation. In general, the more you are requesting that the other invest in satisfying your desires, the more difficult will be your task in getting the goal accomplished. Again, the investment is the cost to the target, not the cost to yourself. Thus one tactic is to plan political activities in ways as they require only small requests from others, or at least requests that are not disproportionate with the value of the investment to you.

One way to do this is to see if you can break the task down into smaller steps. This would have been an alternative that would have served Margaret well. Or, see if it is not possible to spread the cost of the requests around to others.

The Means versus the Ends

For those who think power is a dirty word, then political action may seem like dirty laundry. But all of us use political action in one form or another, and some of us are quite masterful at it. When you influence your spouse to clean up the garage, you are engaging in a political act. You plead. You cajole. You make promises. You structure the situation so that he has no alternative choices. When you finally put your foot down and say, "No sex until you clean up the garage," what is that but a political act?

All the actions we take are, in one form or another, political. The question is whether the means that we choose—our actions—are appropriate to the ends or outcomes we hope to achieve. If you sleep with someone to get promoted, that act is generally considered illegitimate. The means do not suit the ends. But if you legalize your relationship in the form of a marriage, and if you are coowners and partners in the same buisness, is such an act also illegitimate?

Planning political action requires not only that you evaluate the costs to your self and to others but also that you assess the legitimacy of your actions. When all is said and done, will it be worth it to achieve your goal? Will this act enhance your credibility and reputation, or will it diminish it in some way?

The answers to these questions must be well considered before you move forward. Ideally, political battles should be carefully picked and chosen according to the evolving power distributions in the firm, because ultimately your chances of success will be externally controlled. If not, when the dust settles, you may win some interpersonal battles only to ultimately lose the war of politics, due to shifting power distributions in the firm.

And so we come full circle. Dependence is subjectively created while power is externally controlled. And politics, and the manifestation of political acts, simply are what individuals do to restore the power balance. Because no one wants to be powerless. We all want to be in control. Or so we think.

PART **II**

*WHY PEOPLE HAVE A HARD
TIME GETTING THINGS DONE
AND WHAT TO DO ABOUT IT*

From the outset, we have said this book is about why great ideas fail at the hands of smart people. And, we have said the answer is both simple and hard: Simple, because the underpinnings of failure have to do with aspects of organizations that are not merely random, or haphazard, and hard for the same reason—because ideas must either succeed or fail not based on their own merit, the merit of the idea, but within a context. That context is defined increasingly by resources and dependencies at lateral levels, over which managers typically have little formal authority. Even when managers do have formal authority, the ever-dynamic reality of external and internal power and the politics that control organizational resources and their allocation make it challenging to accomplish ideas, objectives, and the best-laid initiatives.

It is hard for another reason. It is hard to be successful when working within complex contexts over which you hold no formal control or authority, because the tools that typically may serve us well in interpersonal relationships and in accomplishing objectives as individuals frequently are inadequate (and sometimes even counterproductive) within the framework of complicated and unfamiliar contexts. Witness, for example, in our first case, how an accomplished chief operating officer fails when she attempts to implement a new managerial philosophy by typical management "methods," against the backdrop of a defensive union; or, the story of a smart and careful Big Five tax manager and his failure to implement an information system promising million-dollar savings.

Our goal in this section is not just to present interesting and pervasive scenarios but to demonstrate solutions. We have come full circle in our discussion of power and lateral relationships. We demonstrate how to understand, and even how to "see" these relationships, arguing although there is an endless stream of political actions occurring everyday in our work places, we have the tools both to understand and to manage these actions.

In Chapters 4, 5, and 6, we considered the strategies and tools of planning political actions. We have argued that such planning requires the same rigor as solving any problem. And, we said it is possible to define a modestly finite set of strategies and actions applicable to a wide variety of difficult problems. Every day, there are thousands of political relationships activated, escalated, and evolving in today's organizations. Within these myriad of activities, however, we have presented tools for managers to take discernible and limited actions.

Even as complexity within political relationships can be distilled to a manageable framework, we have found that the political scenarios can also be distilled to a relatively limited number of very pervasive themes, despite the variance in detail. Chances are you already have come across or have been involved in a situation similar to the vignettes we have presented by way of illustration. It is because these scenarios of power and politics are redundant in organizational life.

In the course of teaching and consulting about organizational dilemmas over the past ten years, we have asked over a thousand M.B.A. students to recount their own political dilemmas. From their hundreds of cases, we have found that certain themes are redundant. So pervasive are these themes that we have categorized the overwhelming majority of "cases" into six major themes to provide a basis for applying both the theory and tools and the ABC model of solving complicated lateral problems.

Themes of business-idea failures are not random. This is a ray of encouraging hope; we may, in fact become more effective in our work places simply by applying this template to common everyday problems that previously have stymied us. Certain themes or motifs repeat over and over every day in our workplaces. These themes have an infinite variety of characters, relationships, desired outcomes, and contexts. This means they can be deciphered as themes that repeat, and thus a certain template can be applied toward solving them.

In the six chapters that follow, we present these six, most pervasive themes.

In Chapter 7, we present a few cases from our work in solving intractable problems. The first concerns a physician trying to implement an improved system of patient care at a psychiatric hospital. In our more detailed strategic case, in which we pull together the concepts and tactics of solving these types of dilemmas, we present the case of Lisa, a hospital chief operating officer. She has authority but not real power in attempting to implement Total Quality Management in a hospital setting. Her plan precipitates a union strike. In this case from our consulting practice, we work toward solving this dilemma as a prototype for managing subordinate and lateral dependencies. We demonstrate how to diagnose real dependencies within the hospital's internal and external context.

In Chapter 8, the cases build on the first set in Chapter 7 and demonstrates how managers' great ideas may fail, even when top level support is achieved. We illustrate several scenarios including a military situation, wherein a lieutenant was ineffective, and demonstrate how reliance upon authority, even in a military context, can be deficient if critical dependencies are ignored. For more detailed analysis, we develop the case of Tod, a Big Six (now Big Five) tax manager, and his attempt to implement an information system. In these cases good ideas affect others adversely, even by costing them their jobs. Providing detailed analysis of how to manage the critical lateral relationships within a business, where relationships are the business and critical resource, we demonstrate how to solve such situations as Tod's, which is applicable to other enterprises as well.

Chapter 9 provides a comparison of failed and successful implementation of good ideas. The first case of Alison, a savvy international business woman, and the next case of a middle-level manager whom we call Ray represent smart people failing. Both are representative of a common motif in organizations: having lots of responsibility, and even a modicum of support from the top, but lacking authority to command those at lateral levels. This problem frequently surprises and frustrates managers because with appropriate authority, they believe successful implementation of their ideas would follow.

Our two core cases compare Ray, a manager in charge of designing, coordinating, and implementing a safety plan at a large manufacturing plant with a successful management of lateral processes. The "success" case is from our client who accomplished an effective process change at a semiconductor firm. This incident involved four plants and off-site manufacturing as well as a deeply entrenched culture which resists change. The person who implemented this small but politically complex change was a student in our Executive Education M.B.A. class at the time of this innovation. Through detailed planning and effective lateral relationship management of dozens of individuals, his process of change was successful and provided a million-dollar savings per year.

Chapter 10 is devoted to highlighting cases about being on the "receiving" side of powerful relationships. Often misdiagnosed as abusive situations, these cases highlight how losing situations often result from failure to understand the dynamics involving lateral relationships and networks. We discuss several cases which bordered on career disaster involving telecommunications, engineering, and international banking. In most cases, what people label as an intractable or unyielding boss has more to do with the structural aspects of the system or situation. Two typical "abusive" situations are highlighted here. One we call the case of being assigned the losing horse (or project), and the other we dub a "power shifting while you weren't looking" dilemma—both pervasive, but manageable.

We close the case section in Chapter 11 by highlighting several cases involving top-level managers to illustrate how being at the top is still about successful lateral-network management. In the first case, a treasurer of a board of directors is foiled when his recommendations are offset by others. In the second, we illustrate a case of "power failure." In this situation, a powerful and highly regarded CEO is at the reigns of an organization, only to fall rapidly from power due to an inability to manage his oblique relationships. Our case section concludes with an illustration of a successful CEO who managed to accomplish an effective organizational turnaround. This individual illustrates well our theory and template of managing lateral and oblique relationships.

We have found that most managerial "failures" fall into the categories discussed in this next section of our book. In each, we present some of the cases and, in each chapter, one detailed case solution. Our analysis encompasses the theoretical first part of this book, by illustrating how to diagnose resources, critical dependencies, and relative context. Next, we provide an analysis of the ABCs and illustrate how to diagram the relationships. Finally, from the set of strategies and tactics denoted in Chapters 5 and 6, we consider the finite set of actions available to actors in any situation. Our overarching goal here is to show you how to think about some seemingly intractable problems, and we propose to solve most of them.

7

The Case of "Your Good Idea Disrupts Another's Power"

One thing managers know is that good ideas often meet resistance. More than a few good ideas and untold numbers of managers have been left stymied when their perfectly sensible ideas have unwittingly interfered with someone else's power. In fact, this scenario is one of the most common themes we have encountered in the past ten years and is one of the most pervasive reasons why good ideas fail. We call this theme "a good idea that steps on somebody's power base."

All managers have seen this before. A well-intended person or manager proposes or tries to enact a good idea, plan, agenda, or proposal in a firm. The good idea meets what many managers call "resistance." The well-meaning managers then work hard to overcome the resistance, all the while creating more ill will and more resistance. Very soon, the resistance is viewed as a personal conflict, sometimes dubbed a "personality conflict."

At some point, the manager calls for help, either in the form of a consultant or a higher-up, or the manager works to fight the resistance by using some means of his or her authority. If personal authority is lacking, the person or manager may evoke a higher level of authority. The authority may be sufficient to offset the resistance or the resistance is coopted or quieted, and the manager's plan or idea is forced into place. The naive consider this a "win," while the seasoned realize this "win" will be short lived, and/or implementation will be half-hearted.

We have seen this situation repeat so often that we include it here. But, we don't call it overcoming resistance, because we think the term "resistance" is both vague and overstated and leads to a variety of actions that are counterproductive.

Resistance has many forms. One repetitive form is when the good idea truly does interfere with another person or group's essential power base. In the case of Jeff in Chapter 6, trying in vein to have his new course proposal accepted, the problem was a political one. Jeff had a good idea, and he had some benchmarking data to support the idea that a new course in entrepreneurship had merit. As we discussed, the committee disliked the course proposal because essentially it interfered with their own power base.

As this book has highlighted, power is about resources and about control over resources. The resources affected in that case include the critical resources of status, reputation, routines, and time. The group of professors had established the courses to be taught and had established reputations around their stellar ideas. To admit that the courses they taught were outdated cost them status, particularly because they themselves hadn't realized it. Because of this, their reputations were challenged.

The younger professors who opposed the new course introduction were concerned about their routines being altered. And, the idea imposed upon their vital resource of time, because it might cost them to develop their own new course structures. All in all, one new course went by the wayside, along with the enthusiasm of the young turk who brought the idea forward, because the idea cost someone else power.

This theme takes so many forms. We have seen it repeat literally dozens of times, thwarting the smartest and brightest. Such scenarios don't merely occur in unstructured environments, in which the chain of command is arguably a bit vague, but often present themselves in highly structured environments and in scenarios where the cost of the good idea and its failure is quite high.

THE CASE OF THE DOCTORS AND THE NEW MEDICAL DIAGNOSTIC SYSTEM

As this book goes to press, many report our health-care system is at a crisis stage. This is what David, an M.D. in the M.B.A. program thought also. Being very smart about the inner workings of health care and very worried at the same time about the financial crisis his urban-based psychiatric hospital was going through, David had developed a thoughtful plan that if executed would be a major cost savings and provide better patient care.

In the facility, diagnoses of psychiatric disorders were being made in ways that prolonged the patient's length of stay in the psychiatric facility. There were four divisions within the facility: one for eating disorders; one for substance abuse; one for serious psychosis; and one for the diagnoses of neuroses for which patients could be treated on an ongoing, out-patient basis. Based on the patients' initial diagnoses, they were categorized into one of the four areas, which would determine treatment for the patient. David realized two problems with this system. As a physician, he realized that problems often overlapped. For example, patients who presented with substance disorders had other problems, and those with an eating disorder, could not easily transfer to other parts of the facility. The result was inadequate care. He realized that the practice was creating reputation problems within the community for this facility, whose patients and families were often frustrated by fragmented care. Their frustration was shared by some of the hospital staff, who saw what was sometimes called the "revolving-door patient"—that is, patients are treated, but return over and over because the underlying problems aren't solved. In the process, these patients run out of insurance reimbursement. The hospital, being knowledgeable about the patients and sometimes even their suicidal tendencies is obligated to readmit and to treat such revolving-door patients, for both ethical and legal reasons.

David's plan was to set up a system wherein patients could be seen by physicians and staff in any one of the four divisions, depending on internal consultation and as their symptoms warranted. This he believed would provide more comprehensive care to the patients and reduce the numbers of revolving-door admissions. At the same time, it would predictably help the hospital in the longer run, as patients without insurance would require fewer charitable care readmissions. Since this would affect the hospital's bottom line, David thought his proposal would win quick approval.

What David failed to realize however was that the division's resources were tied to a measure called acuity. In hospitals, acuity refers to the patients and the severity of their diagnoses. Here, each division received reimbursement based on the numbers of patients and their diagnoses. Each division's staffing was also allocated based on the severity of their patients. This was a matter of diagnosis. David's plan was thus better for the patient, their families, and long-term prognoses. It was also better for the hospital in the long term, as the hospital overall was losing money because reimbursement wasn't sufficient to cover the cost of chronic readmissions. But the division heads blocked David's well-written proposal. This great proposal impacted too much on their own resource base. Simply put, while saving the hospital money, it cost the doctors.

David's proposal failed. Neither his hard earned knowledge of medicine nor his business acumen had prepared him for this political pitfall. Had David counted the real costs of both money and precedent, and executed his plan accordingly, we think he could have succeeded. In hindsight, so did David. But, more important, David was not alone.

Dozens of this type of scenario inflate our files, as similarly smart and motivated people attempt to improve their organizational worlds.

We turn now to solving a dilemma in detail, pulling together the concepts of the early chapters of this book and the strategies, tactics, and model for planning and executing effective political action. As the theme repeats, we believe, so also might the solution.

A HOSPITAL CHIEF OPERATING OFFICER AND THE UNION

In this case, a newly appointed hospital chief operating officer, whom we will call Lisa, faced a challenge when her smartly designed Total Quality Management (TQM) proposal faced opposition from the hospital union. Several years ago, one of the authors of this book received a frantic call from Lisa. Only three months into her new appointment as chief operating officer in a local community hospital, Lisa had plenty to worry about. The hospital's service employee union was threatening to strike. Worse, the union was blaming the new operating officer's "great idea" of pushing TQM as a key reason precipitating the strike.

Union problems were hardly new to Lisa. She had worked at XYZ hospital for ten years, having worked her way through the ranks as a nurse and then as department manager and coordinator. She always considered herself a friend of the union and empathetic of their rights to retain hard-earned privileges, such as pay scales and membership drives. As a nurse, she had even seriously entertained pushing unionization among the nurses. The last time the union went on strike ended up being hard on the hospital's business because the local community was well connected to the union and had supported their point of view.

But now Lisa was in administration. She felt outraged that the union would take such a stance. Beyond her outrage, Lisa was baffled. "Why didn't the union want TQM?" she asked us. Maybe her fellow administrators were right about the union workers when they argued that they just didn't get it and would fight most administrative proposals. Maybe, she thought, they couldn't understand the merits of TQM.

Armed with this insight, Lisa's first step at "countering the resistance" was to set up a meeting with the union's leadership to show them clearly how valuable a TQM program would be to the hospital. She saw TQM as a philosophy that would counter some of the hospital's problems Lisa had identified while doing a project course in our M.B.A. curriculum. Some of the problems Lisa had identified were the lack of interdepartmental coordination within the hospital and a "backward" focused attitude. This she felt was because of a culture that did not support teamwork and in which new and innovative ideas were usually discouraged before they were understood. People blamed people for problems; departments blamed departments; and the hospital was developing a bad rap in its local community for patient errors.

Spurred on by a consultant friend, Lisa saw TQM as a philosophy that could change the hospital. As the consultant had pontificated, "TQM will help you to build teams in your organization. It will enable your employees to identify and solve problems themselves. It will allow you to identify processes where high error rates exist or where waste is evident. Mostly, it will empower individuals and bring new creativity to the hospital."

Added to the merits of the philosophy was a simple reality: Lisa was aware that many hospitals in her state were beginning TQM efforts to address issues such as medication errors and patient care. Hospitals without TQM programs in place were being viewed negatively by the state hospital accreditation board. So, she felt that implementing a TQM program would not only address some of the hospitals major problems, but would have the side benefit of helping her to win points with the hospital board of directors, who supported her proposal.

In short, Lisa was sold on the TQM philosophy and had already signed a contract with the consultant who had promised a comprehensive TQM program for a reasonable fee. Lisa and the consultant had worked to design a custom-made program, with implementation plans for involving all departments of the hospital. Lisa was particularly proud of her own input in developing the program for training the union employees. Convinced that empowerment was consistent with union philosophy, Lisa began holding meetings with union leaders to convince them of the merits of the total quality improvement effort. Now, a month later, the union was threatening to strike and the reason was TQM.

Lisa was aghast. "I just don't get it," she complained. "This program promotes the importance of employees, and especially service employees, by promoting empowerment. It highlights employee input in decision making. It provides 5 percent of the work week for training in brainstorming, being heard, and making a difference. Isn't this the same philosophy as Gus, the union leader promotes?" she asked. "Why is the union upset about total quality management, which I designed with union interests at heart?"

Why indeed? The idea of implementing a hospital-wide TQM program clearly had merit. Even the planning—involving the union leaders in selling the program and training—would score points on most case analyses in M.B.A. school. So, why was the union threatening to strike? What did Lisa do wrong?

Although you may have already realized how Lisa was naive to discount the very real power of the union, her mistakes tend to be repeated by very smart individuals trying to make an impact on their work places.

Lisa subscribed to typical myths about power. These myths dominated her actions and rendered her ineffective.

Myth One: Focus on the Merits of the Idea

Like many smart managers, Lisa was focused on the merits of the idea itself. In fact, the main reason why this theme of "good ideas stepping on other people's power" repeats over and over is because the tendency to focus on our own ideas and agendas is extraordinarily prevalent. There is nothing wrong with that. Points are won for arguing a position and sticking with it—right? There is just one problem. The focus on the idea also causes us to *ignore the context* within which those ideas must be accepted. When we hit resistance, the tendency is to focus all the more on the merits of the idea and to push that idea more diligently.

And that is what Lisa did. When push comes to shove, as it often does with new innovative ideas, she pushed. They shoved, and she pushed again, in a slightly more polished fashion. Lisa wouldn't have called it pushing; rather she used her best communication skills and influence tactics. She put together a presentation, designed to demonstrate the merits of TQM.

Myth Two: "Surely They Will See It"

Like we all sometimes do, Lisa was enamored with her own agenda. We find support for those agendas, programs, proposals, plans, and ideas much as Lisa did with the consultant. When others don't buy into our ideas, we see the problem as "them." We hold meetings, try out influence tactics and engage in all sorts of activities designed with one goal in mind: to get "them" to see "it"—with "them" being those who resist and "it" being our point of view, program, plan, or idea. This is why negotiations often go awry. Despite well-intended negotiations, the aim is still to get our own ideas and agendas across. Even if it means a little compromise, we are giving up just a portion of our own idea or agenda, rather than viewing the larger perspective.

Myth Three: Use Authority to Push an Idea and Overcome Resistance

Like many managers, Lisa used her authority to push the idea. "They don't see it or get it" means push harder, using one's authority, and all of its privileges to get the idea across. In this situation, the consultant was called back in to muster more credibility and legitimacy for the plan. The consultant ended up trying to meet with the union to make the plan legitimate from the outside and also to facilitate cooperation. This just made the union angrier, as they saw through the intended cooptation.

Some management experts advocate this as "overcoming resistance." They argue that the driving forces for change must be made clear and the resisting forces against change overcome. In our estimation, this is the mindset that leads to layoffs, strikes, or passive–aggressive resistance.

In this case, when the idea hit resistance, Lisa pushed harder. The union pushed back harder. Each side reemphasized their own beliefs and agendas. The union became entrenched in the view that management indeed didn't care, and Lisa, along with her cohort of administrators, were further strengthened in their view that the union was indeed intractable.

Let's step back from this power battle and diagnose the context and the nature of the power within the lateral relationships in this business, as we have discussed throughout this book, and ask a few questions:

- Who has the power in this context?
- How is the power distributed?
- What resources are at stake here?
- What are the critical dependencies?
- What is the context within which the idea must find acceptance?

Examining the Context: Who Holds Power?

When proposing new ideas in organizations, the most common mistake is to ignore the affect of that idea on the various groups or departments outside of one's own immediate bailiwick. That was the case with Margaret and the information system gone awry. When one group is upset about a new idea or plan, it's a pretty safe bet that someone's power base has been threatened. And power is almost always about control over resources or dependencies. That is exactly what happened here. We'll take a look at the resources and dependencies here to understand the power issues and then turn to "solving" the case: The case of a good idea disrupts another group's power base.

Resources and Dependencies in the Hospital Industry

Stepping back from the immediate conflict we have to ask, What are the resources that are essential in the hospital industry and in this hospital in particular within its place in the larger industry? In today's world, patients and the money they or their insurance companies pay to the hospitals are the most important external resources. Internally, the hospital needs staff, doctors, nurses, and increasingly, the nonprofessional staff who provide patient care and services. In today's world of hospital changes, administrators come and go. Because of a decline in hospital in-patient stays and the supply of medical doctors, in some regions the collective power of doctors as well as the power of administrators has declined.

The hospital is absolutely dependent on a steady stream of patients. This particular hospital exists on the outskirts of a large city with many hospitals. Its reputation in the community for patient service is one of the only differentiating features it has. Its patients, in short, have many choices of hospitals. And, the doctors and nurses have many choices for their services as well. If we look a little closer at the context (something very difficult for managers to do, especially once the conflict has become personalized), we can note that this hospital is a community hospital. About 75 percent of its business is local—very local. Further, about 80 percent of its service employees live in the immediate area. Why is this information about context vital? As you've probably realized by now, a strong network exists between the union employees and the community—between the union and the hospital's vital dependency or its "customers." This is why this particular union is capable of shutting down the hospital and keeping all but the sickest, emergency-room patients away from it.

That is exactly what the union has done in the past. Lisa didn't see this critical piece of the context and relied heavily, as many newly minted M.B.A.s do, on her idea, her own authority, and clout as "boss." The reality is, the union has more power over the hospital's critical dependencies and resources than Lisa has. And worse for Lisa—the union membership knows it and she doesn't. She is working with her pie charts and flipcharts to demonstrate the merits of an idea, without any understanding of context. The union members understand their power in context and Lisa's naiveté. This is a bad combination for a new hospital administrator.

Power Distribution

We've discussed why the union holds the external controlled power of the organization. But why has TQM threatened its power and resource base? TQM per se is not an evil or inherently threatening concept. We won't rehearse all of its nuances here, but on its own, it is pretty sensible stuff. It has been a popular managerial philosophy with practical applications throughout the 1980s and 1990s. But, resources exist in context, and so a look at context is a critical first step. In this scenario, the union has little power over wages. During a time in which union solidarity is relatively weak, and union membership has plateaued, the union is struggling to maintain its identity. What does it offer to new members? It has relatively little leverage over benefits and little control or power over scheduling, hours, or even layoffs, which were widespread in this particular town in the early 1990s. What is the union's power? Its core power is in identity—an ideology, a sense of solidarity, sense of empowerment, a voice in a time when voice and contribution are increasingly invisible. Now that we have done the critical dependency and resource analysis and have a clearer sense of the relationship and power components of the context, we can turn to a few more specific questions.

Costs to the Target

This brings us to critical question of what the TQM program costs the union. In short, the problem with the TQM program was that it threatened the union by appearing to replicate the union's core philosophy. By threatening to take over the union's core ideology, management appeared to be offering something that would replace the union. In essence, this nifty management ideology was threatening the very core identity and purpose of the union. The union feared, and perhaps quite understandably so, that the TQM program would be a perfect substitute for its own agenda. Like any substitute product or very spiffy competitor, TQM deserved to be treated as a very real threat. The union also was sufficiently savvy to draw upon past sentiment toward managerial intervention and distrusted anything new which promised greater employee voice, having interpreted such past efforts as a trick.

As we have argued throughout this book, solving political dilemmas requires careful analysis and mindful recognition of very difficult issues. Now that some of the essential issues have been thought through, we can turn to solving the case. We begin with a diagram of the political relationships—the ABCs—to more clearly "see" the options available to Lisa (see Figure 7.1).

The ABC Analysis

Diagramming the ABCs is a good first step for planning political action, because it forces a conscious consideration of the actors, targets, context, and what is desired as an outcome. As we diagram the key actors and context of this case, several issues become clear. In addition to context issues, we see that other players are relevant, beyond the immediate agent (A) and target (B). There are, for example, other agents who may also benefit from the TQM implementation; and there are other targets whom Lisa may want to consider, such as the community who

Figure 7.1
Lisa and the Total Quality Management Program

X = A wants to implement a TQM program.
X′ = A wants to advance her reputation.

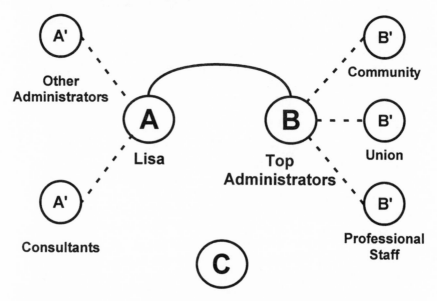

Organization Context = Union has strong community support and has effectively struck before. Union membership is on the decline. TQM threatens the union's power.

may benefit from an increased focus on customer satisfaction and her nonunionized staff who may appreciate the philosophy of TQM.

The diagram also helps to clarify the X—a realization of what an actor may want, in addition to that which is stated or immediately conscious. In this case, the X was the TQM program, but if we look to what is needed by Lisa, behind what she wants, we can see that a good reputation and future clout as an administrator are what she really wants. We diagram this into the equation as the X prime.

This is the case with many a new manager. The focus is on a program or idea because (1) they are so eager to right the wrongs they have seen while advancing into management; (2) it is a legitimate, sensible endeavor; or (3) it will serve as a vehicle for advancing their reputations. The program becomes the focus, but what they really want and need is to be known as effective and defined as having done a good job at solving the organization's problems, as well as to receive accolades from their peers and applause from their higher-ups. This motivation has spurred many a new program. When resistance is met, as it often is with the politically naive, or even the well-seasoned manager, the overwhelming tendency is for the program to become the focus. The means become the end, so to speak.

Action Planning for Effective Political Action

What capabilities and actions are open to A? In Chapter 5 of this book, we laid out the potential actions available to actors within a political relationship, in which they face a power imbalance and seek to remedy it. We said that those actions include a fairly limited set of options. More specifically, they include

- Paying the tax.
- Expanding the search: Look for support beyond the immediate target.
- Building coalition—either with available A prime or B prime.
- Affecting the context.
- Ignoring the dependency and solving the dilemma alone.
- Changing the desire or X.

These are essentially the set of actions available to Lisa or any other individual who is trying to implement an innovative idea in a political situation. Let's examine these alternatives within the context of this scenario.

Paying the Tax

Lisa could pay the tax the union wants—that is, she could acquiesce to their demand to drop the TQM program, acknowledging that it interferes with their essential membership issues. She could give up the idea and some power and let the union win. That has a big cost. The cost to her is her reputation. The failure would be known and likely viewed as a failure by the hospital board. If she were clever, she might be able to obtain some reciprocal concessions from the union, but this is unlikely, given the power imbalance and the sense of win–lose that is likely to come from this failure.

Expanding the Search: Look for Support beyond the Immediate Target

Here, Lisa has some leverage as illustrated in the ABC diagram. She needs to ask a few questions: Who are the alternate targets in this case? Moreover, what is their likely interest in promoting her cause? She might find some support that would be sufficient to advance her agenda with B prime, in this case, the staff and professionals in the hospital who are nonunion members, by focusing on improved patient care. Or, she might consider another B prime, such as enlisting influential community members who might promote the interest externally or be able to affect prominent union members.

In this case, there is some risk to evoking community support for TQM. One potential consequence would be to evoke distrust from the union, which holds the power in this context. The strategy of building support beyond the immediate targets might backfire in this scenario. An agent planning political action may eventually rule out certain B primes, however, we find it helpful to list as many possible targets as is reasonable in an effort to expand options and explore potential "levers" for action. In essence, in the planning stage, an agent should list potential targets and count the costs and likelihood of support from those targets, as well as the consequences. In most cases, we find new options for action become apparent, via this method of expanding the search. Here, the nonunion staff, administrators, and physicians may be appropriate targets who could begin and model TQM programs.

Build a Coalition

Building a coalition for one's idea or agenda involves first of all a careful consideration of the available agents and targets. As we discussed in detail in Chapter 6, the agent needs to consider the costs and the likelihood of support from the potential agents and targets. Often, this type of political action is highly effective. In the hospital case, the alternate agents include the community and the professional staff. Their support could help to make this a hospital-wide effort, rather than just the new manager's program.

Coalition building involves giving away some of the ownership of an idea or plan and temporarily the power. Smart people sometimes avoid doing so because they become quite wedded to "their" plans or ideas. However, by sharing the power, the responsibility is spread, and the network is enhanced, as commitment to the new agenda spreads. Often, it is far more difficult for decision makers to turn down a coalition, for some rather obvious but often ignored reasons. To turn down a group of supporters might cost a decision maker goodwill multiplied many times over.

Affect the Context

The fourth available option is to affect the context: the C in our model of political relationships. To do so means being knowledgeable of the context, which unfortunately is something people forget as they become zealous about the merits of the idea itself.

In this case, we have said that the union holds strong community influence because a majority of the hospital staff lives in the immediate community, which comprises the hospital's catchment area. Our agent, in her initial plan, had ignored this external control aspect and downplayed the capability of this union to affect the community and the hospital's business. The power of the union in the community was the first aspect of this situation we worked with in reshaping the situation.

Our plan involved reshaping the TQM program, quieting the immediate conflict by backing off from this program. Later, we worked with the essential aspects of this program Lisa wanted, working with the benefits to the union and the community in reframing the idea.

Change the Desire or X

This plan brought into play the final option, which is often the last one to be considered by those whose ideas take over their capability to plan for the idea's success. This option is last in our list. That is because it is often the last thing a new manager thinks about, so focused are they on getting the idea or agenda across. Also, in today's society, changing what we want or promote is sometimes viewed as a sign of weakness or antithetical to the paradigm of a manager as controller and in control.

Yet, in many scenarios, this option is the most sensible and often carries the lowest cost. We think it is the best strategy for this type of scenario, where the power is currently so imbalanced that the idea itself is unlikely to succeed, even if coalitions of support are obtained or alternate targets cultivated. Also, once coalitions of resistance have been formed, as in this case, and the idea has become lost in the conflict, it is sensible to stop and rethink the X—what is really wanted in the long term? This question is essential to keep from the proverbial and devastating "winning the battle but losing the war" script.

So what is the real X, or thing wanted, here? What Lisa really wants is to improve patient care; build supportive teams; give employees a sense of empowerment; assess antiquated processes that are leading to poor patient care; and, in the long haul, improve customer satisfaction. She also wants to demonstrate to the Occupational Safety and Health Administration (OSHA) that her hospital is not ignoring new technology or patient safety concerns. And, most importantly and hardest to admit, what she really wants is her own sense of success, measured by her peers, and by her new CEO, seeing her as an innovative and effective manager. She could accomplish these same objectives without the rhetoric of a program agenda. More important, she could accomplish them far more effectively with the support of, rather than the antagonism of, one of her core dependencies.

Lessons of the Case

How could Lisa have preempted the adverse union reaction? Afterall, she did not intend to trick them; she was sincere about providing a program that would be good for the union and the hospital.

One simple thing Lisa might have done is what all planners should do: Think about whose interests are at stake with a new plan. In this case, she might have considered the union as a group and asked the same question about the union she might have posed about all the stakeholders: What is their resource base? What is their source of power? Considering how this new plan affects that resource base and power would have served Lisa well.

New plans and ideas by definition almost always replace old plans, old processes, and ways of doing the work. Whose interests are likely to be affected? This is an important question to pose. More commonly, people who teach change or plan change promote asking the question, Whose support is needed? That is not quite the right question. It's a start, and certainly one level beyond the question, What's the task or plan? But real effectiveness in managing lateral relationships involves much more than this. It begins with a careful consideration of the interests at stake.

The Solution: What Actions Should Lisa (the Agent) Take?

We recommend Lisa should act upon the ABCs of the political relationship and the realities of the context, the cost, and the dependencies. We believe that she, like other managers caught in situations where they discover their good idea has interfered with a powerful group, should do the following to plan and take action:

1. Do the resource dependency analysis—realize who has the power and work within that reality.
2. Do an analysis of the larger context to understand and work with the resistance.
3. Diagram the relationship to "see" more precisely who is a player, what levers may be pushed, and what one's own essential interests are.
4. Be very clear and thoughtful about what exactly you want and what it will cost you. Define the X to be mindful of long-term and short-term interests.
5. Go through the list of available actions available to all agents in a political relationship.
6. Choose the option and combination of options that works, given the analysis.
7. Execute the action with detailed planning and as much rigor as any other problem or endeavor.

For Lisa, in the face of hostile reaction to the TQM program and in this context of union leverage, we advocate carefully considering X—what is really wanted. Lisa can accomplish all the objectives of TQM without calling this a formal program with the hostility it has evoked.

CONCLUSION

We have presented this pervasive theme in detail because, simply put, people want to accomplish their great ideas. And they often fail to consider how their ideas impact others. This was the case with Jeff and his new course failure. As we discussed in Chapter 6, in presenting the target side of perception, Jeff was left bewildered. "There's nothing wrong with this new course proposal," he insisted. And he was right. He simply succumbed to the great myths of great ideas—focusing on the idea rather than the context and the merits of the idea, and rather than the resource cost to those who must implement them.

David the M.D. had a good idea which would have resulted in a formidable cost savings and represented an improvement to patient and customers alike. This plan too went to "good-idea heaven," for he was unable to recognize the way his plan affected the resource base of significant others. As it posed a threat to the assets of other physicians in the various divisions of the psychiatric hospital, David's plan went unrealized. Merit and cost savings aside, the plan lost in the political arena of lateral relationships.

Finally, Lisa's great idea of introducing TQM represents an ideology and change which threatened the very group it was designed to help. We have seen this theme of a good and even great idea impacting other's power bases (and thus failing) in dozens of variations. The players, situations, and specifics change, but the underlying theme remains the same. That is why these themes can be analyzed. Being effective in executing ideas and plans is not a "soft" game. Rather, there is a template for thinking about the idea in context and a finite set of options to consider and execute.

In our next case, we look at one further variation of the great idea impacts power theme. In Chapter 8, we examine the case of Tod, a smart, accomplished tax manager at a large consulting firm, and his dilemma in implementing a new automated system. Like Lisa, Tod had a great idea that would be useful for solving important problems in his firm. Unlike Lisa, Jeff, and David, Tod's plan had very strong internal support from the people at the top. It was an idea that had authority behind it, but it unraveled in its execution.

8

The Case of "Your Good Idea Costs Others Their Jobs"

One of the key reasons great ideas fail is because they impact others adversely. Quite often, the proponents of innovative ideas, agendas, and systems are clueless about their effects. In the case of Lisa in Chapter 7, the new TQM program clearly impacted the union's power base by threatening to directly compete with that which made the union strong. This smart but somewhat naive chief operating officer chose to advance her agenda without considering its effect. And with little understanding of opposition's real power, she thought her authority would carry the day. This situation repeats itself every day in American business, much to the consternation of smart managers.

Smart managers trying to advance their projects often become baffled when their plans are not well received, and all the more so when the source of resistance arises from those at lateral levels within the organization, as we saw with Dr. Dave. It's even worse when their great idea is quite consistent with the firm's mission and fully in line with the organization's overarching goals as both Lisa and Dave's plans were.

The two cases that follow are from the experiences of innovative managers who had top management support for their initiatives and sufficient personal authority to achieve success. In each case, the initiatives were impeded by their colleagues and subordinates. In the first case of Lieutenant Tom, we demonstrate that even military orders are not always sufficient for obtaining lateral support. In the second, for which we develop a solution according to the ABC analysis, we draw on the case of our client, Tod, who was a tax manager in a Big Six (now Big Five) consulting firm.

TOM AND THE MILITARY

Tom was a newly commissioned officer stationed in the U.S. Army in Germany and charged with maintaining the training equipment for his division. Upon arriving at his post, he found the equipment had not been maintained and so it often failed during training events. The battalion commander made Tom aware of the problem with an order to rectify the equipment in short order.

This boded well with Tom, who was quite eager to demonstrate his technical knowledge and capability. The problem captured the attention of Tom's commanding officer, and Tom saw it as politically advantageous as well. Quickly surveying the situation, Tom came up with a detailed maintenance plan aimed at increasing each soldier's awareness of how to care for the equipment. This way, he reasoned, the cost would be upon the soldiers rather than upon their commanding officers. Too, he thought his version of the plan was more likely to succeed because the soldiers would be motivated to care for equipment that they would use.

The structure of the units consisted of a battalion commander, the battalion staff, and five subordinate units, each of whom had a company commander. Tom had worked directly with the battalion and company commanders and had convinced them that the plan would work. After a lengthy briefing with a few minor changes, he got the "order to implement the plan during the next quarter."

The results of how effective he had been would be judged by the success of a large-scale training event to take place in four months. Tom spent the next three months preparing, but the equipment was still malfunctioning. He then had to explain why after being ordered to implement his plan and being given resources to do so, he had failed.

Tom realized upon later analysis of this situation, as an M.B.A. student, that his plan failed based on one critical oversight. In Tom's words, "I believe I failed in accomplishing the assigned mission based on one critical piece of information concerning the organizational structure. While I had worked with and convinced the commanders in the unit, I had failed to enlist the support or even to consider the interests of the officers in the battalion. I ignored these individuals despite the fact that they would be the ones charged with achieving the goals set in my plan."

In short, the real cost of Tom's plan would be to the battalion officers. Tom thought that in a military setup with its clear chain of command and hierarchical structure, "an order" would be sufficient for getting things done. But in hindsight, he realized that he had ignored the very people he had intended to motivate. Sometimes, orders and chain of command without motivation produce a lack-luster response. In Tom's situation, the response was outright resistance.

It is particularly unfortunate to fail early on in one's tenure in an organization. First impressions of leadership or managerial "failures" often have a lasting effect. In this case, the perception of Tom's "leadership" skills took a serious hit. He became known as ineffective and never did regain the trust of his superiors. Tom ended up leaving the military.

We think the pattern of innovation resulting in failure and exit is not a good one. We turn next to outlining how to win in the innovation game.

TOD AND THE TAX INFORMATION SYSTEM

Our next case takes a look at a frustrating but solvable problem experienced by Tod, a talented manager in a Big Six (now Big Five) consulting firm who designed and attempted to implement an automated system. His plan met the organizational goals but not the organizational realities. It could have saved the firm millions and had top-level support and resources, but it unraveled at the critical level of lateral relationships.

We include it because more than in most such cases, Tod seemed on the surface to do so many things right. He had a plan that was not something he cooked up as a brainy idea, but divorced from the corporation's mission. This plan was a good one. It was consistent with the corporation's goals. And, it had a clear implementation strategy and detailed, specific actions. Better yet, it actually involved the right people to support it. Good idea, demonstrable cost savings, right timing, good implementation planning, detailed and specific actions, right people involved with money to back development—what went wrong?

The Consulting Business

To paint the context of Tod's innovation involves a short summary of the tax-consulting business. Like many tax firms, this large firm has two major lines of business; the consulting business and the compliance business. The latter is mostly routine work and covers the tax returns that clients must file with various tax authorities. A formidable amount of competition had developed for this service because this process recurs pretty routinely year after year. To differentiate itself from the burgeoning competition, from both large and venture type tax services, Tod's firm had decided that the differentiation would be along the lines of cost.

This strategy had gone over well with its clients, who were price sensitive and viewed compliance as a commodity product that they increasingly bought on the basis of price. Thus there had been tremendous pressure on this firm, as well as the other large accounting consulting firms, to cut costs in the compliance side of their business, while the other arm of the business—consulting—was differentiated by quality over prices.

One problem loomed. The firm found that its compliance arm was in trouble. The amount of time spent on billable hours was approaching real costs because the work was very time intensive. At the same time, clients couldn't fully appreciate the value of this firm's service, which was costing them twice as much as some of the competitors; in some cases clients were becoming less willing to pay for this service.

The solution Tod developed was to automate the labor-intensive functions. As a tax manager, Tod attempted to fix the problem created by competing on cost in a time-intensive service. Keeping with the firm's new mission statement, which included the notion of automating via personal computers, he drew up plans to automate client's financial statement ledgers into the firm's tax preparation software.

The "Textbook Solution"

Believing he held a sound idea whose time had surely come, Tod's first move was to prepare an implementation plan. Before moving an inch, he identified the right people who would need to be involved. He knew he needed support at the top and set out to get it. He carefully prepared a proposal for the audit and tax division managing partners that outlined the program and its purpose, goals, costs, and implementation schedule.

His proposal included a carefully done cost-benefit analysis. This was a sure-fire bet, as the costs to the organization were minimal, with much of the technology already in place. The cost to the clients was minimal as well, ranging from $250 to $500 per client. The net effect for the firm was good. The client cost was roughly equivalent to current costs since clients couldn't appreciate the time-intensive nature of this work. After an approximate six-month learning curve, the firm should start to break even on this work and in time make money from the automated system. Clients should be happy because the work could actually be done more quickly and in some cases more accurately.

Step one was to get the top dogs to approve the plan and give Tod the go-ahead. In addition to their encouraging approval, they gave Tod the full budget he had requested to implement the new system. Tod's mentor went yet a step further and offered his support, in case anybody gave him a rough time.

Step two was to discuss the program with the individual tax managers. These were largely Tod's peers. He was excited to present his system to the managers who, Tod explained, stood much to gain. The real benefits to these managers was that a dramatic reduction in staff hours would result. This was attractive from a financial standpoint because staff hours in the compliance part of the industry were the lowest recovery portion of the practice. Because work could be done faster and more efficiently, the fee recovery rate would improve. Overall, the increased use of technology, better labor efficiency, and lower cost structure for compliance would allow the firm to bid more competitively for other projects. In sum, the managers had much to gain from this process.

The first meeting with the individual managers went well. No one voiced complaints, and there was even some recognition that Tod's plan was "not bad." The support of the managers was important to Tod because they needed to be able to explain the program to their clients and alleviate any client fears about automated records. These managers would also be involved in training their staff in the new system.

The staff were not so happy, but Tod didn't worry. They were the only group who expressed a slight discontent, for the reasons people often dislike new technology. They worried that the new technology would replace their jobs. Some of them were probably right.

From Idea to Support to Implementation

Tod did what a lot of managers do, with perfectly good sense. He counted on his idea, his careful plans, and his careful presentation of the plan to the relevant higher-ups and middle-level managers to result in success. And so it seemed. From there, he began working out the implementation details and processes of putting the new system in place.

Celebrating his victory with a colleague, he vaguely wished the staff weren't disgruntled, but decided that he couldn't worry about that. "No one likes change," he reasoned, "and besides, technology always upsets people who don't fully understand the big picture and how it benefits the firm." His friend reassuringly said, "I wouldn't worry about it, Tod. I've been here through a lot of changes and if the partners want it, it's a go. The managers will take care of their staff—don't worry about that. And if some people have to go, well, hey it's a great job market right now. The bottom line is this technology saves the firm money, and it's a good thing for us. The staff just can't see the big picture. You'll probably be promoted before you know it."

While Tod was savoring his success and busily preparing implementation details, the staff, a large group made up of about sixty college hires with one to five years experience in the firm, were spinning their wheels. They didn't just dislike the plan; they were livid at the threat of job loss. They saw this automated system as something that would cut into their ranks, with some potential job loss, and some also had the compliance side of the practice as a career track and disliked the long-term prospects of this new efficient service.

The staff sought their managers' support to resist this new technology. It didn't take much talking—some of the managers secretly disliked the plan for other reasons. As a group, the managers had been uncomfortable saying so when Tod met with them to describe the new automated system. Tod had presented the plan as a done deal that had the partner's approval. Tod had taken their relatively calm responses and nods, along with a few comments about the automated system, as support.

Unbeknownst to Tod, the other managers had met without him. Clients who knew the firm from their compliance work would often ask for them for other projects, generating other business in the firm. This gave some of the managers a competitive edge. Using their staff's frustration as fuel for their own quieter concerns, the managers and their staff formed a wall of appreciable resistance.

By the second week, after what Tod viewed as "very supportive meetings" with the partners and managers, people were finding ways to avoid Tod. The managers canceled his scheduled implementation planning meeting. By the third week, Tod was called to the general partners' office. Tom was told, "We are putting this project on hold." "Would you like me to gather more data?" Tom asked, anticipating that, as usual, more data would be desirable for some of the more conservative partners to fully appreciate the cost savings. "No, Tom. The project is on hold. We don't think it is feasible after all." When Tom pressed for a reason for this change of heart, the partners explained that Tod had not thought about the consequences of his plan, and they were disappointed with his lack of foresight and wondered openly about his "real" agenda.

What agenda? And what had happened to their enthusiasm and support? Tod knew better than to ask. More than a little embarrassed and not ever sure of what had happened, Tod continued to work as a tax manager in this firm for another six months. He never did resume the same level of trust and friendship with his cohort, the other tax managers, and left the firm to return to graduate school. He told one of the authors of this book that his real interest in getting an M.B.A. was to try to gain better insight into this painfully confusing incident, which remained a confusing blob on his otherwise impressive career track.

The Analysis

We analyzed this case with Tod in our M.B.A. class and here because it illustrates the principles of lateral relationships, power, and politics. It appeared that Tod had followed common business sense, intuition, and very careful planning in trying to move his good idea from the planning stage to reality, and we have seen this theme repeat over and over in different industries with smart people failing, despite excellent ideas, planning, and even top-level support.

For success, we think it is absolutely critical to change our way of thinking about ideas and their implementation. It isn't enough to plan, it isn't enough to have detailed action and implementation plans, and baffling as it may seem, it isn't enough to have support from the top. We will follow our template for successful implementation by looking at the context, the resources, and the dependencies of this industry and firm, as well as the real costs to those who must carry out the plan. Next, we'll develop a strategic action plan by diagramming the ABCs of this intractable problem.

The Context: Resources and Dependencies

As always, the place to begin with successful implementation of a new idea is three steps back—a look at the larger context of the industry and the resources and dependencies that make it tick.

What is the context into which this new system must fit? It's the tax-consulting business. In this case, the firm is in a city with lots of competitors. Historically and culturally, large consulting firms are based on the merit and quality of their client relationships. While partners truly own the firm, their success as partners is based on how successful their people are—specifically their managers.

What are the key resources of the firm? The key resources needed to operate in the consulting arena are money and people. More specifically, money comes from clients and billable hours. The people who are essential are the partners and managers, and the staff to a degree, although in most consulting firms, the staff are viewed as more easily replaceable, as each year many thousands of new recruits with accounting degrees seek positions in these top firms. (In rare years, demand has outstripped supply, but in this particular context, the power is on the side of the tax-consulting firms.)

What are the dependencies of the firm and the key players who manage them? The client relationships are the critical dependency of this business. Who manages those? It's the partners and the managers, and to a supervised extent, the staff. It's that simple. The relationships with clients make or break this firm, relative to its competitors. The critical dependency of the managers is money and how it is earned. In this business, it is billable hours, so anything which impacts billable hours is, by nature of the business (and the dependencies of the actors), going to be suspect. This too is a matter of reputation and client relationships. Now, after thinking through the resources and dependencies of this firm, we can ask the question most "action plans" start with: Whose support is needed and why? Tod needs the support of the managers—they are even more pivotal to the successful implementation of his project than the partners. Further, he must maintain this through understanding their critical dependency, which is their client relationships.

Given the resource-dependency analysis, it is clear why Tod failed. Tod hadn't thought about the reality that the managers were evaluated based on the gross revenue they generated, not on their net revenue. Their rewards were billable hours. If the program were implemented, this would have resulted in a temporary drop in gross revenue, though their net revenue would have increased.

Second, the managers' power and prestige in the firm were directly dependent on the number of staff and senior consultants who worked for them. With automation, this number would diminish at least temporarily, if not permanently. There was a potential risk that some of the managers themselves could be out, as transferring their skills to the more general consulting arm of the firm posed a difficult challenge for the older managers.

Most important, they had reputations to uphold with their clients, whom they viewed in a proprietary way. They didn't like anyone else (most assuredly not junior managers, who were beneath them in corporate hierarchy) to get involved with their clients. Automation would imply substitutability. Anyone could download and work with their client's file, if they should be unavailable, thus cutting into the sacred client relationship, and the power, prestige, and future business it suggested. Tod's program would have changed all of that with new technology threatening to bypass the managers as the knowledge bearers. Simply put, it cut into the manager's source of power. And that in a nutshell is why this program, for all the great planning and intelligent rationale, went belly up.

Lessons of the Case

How could Tod have been more effective in managing this useful new system? Standard recipes for managing change prescribe that we ask whose support is needed. Also, we are encouraged to identify resistance and push the driving forces for change. We offer that this prescription is at best only a small step from complete naiveté. As we discussed in Margaret's case, identifying resistance and pushing against it often encourages more resistance. And, asking whose support is needed is a first step. But, it is simply not enough to ask, whose support is needed? As we see in this case, Tod did this. Identifying targets is important, but only as a first step and as part of a more careful strategic and tactical planning effort.

ABC Analysis

From the ABC diagram in Figure 8.1, we see a few aspects of this situation more clearly. The diagram identifies the key targets and potential alternate agents. It provides a framework for thinking about the context, and it provides more clarity about what Tod as the key agent actually wanted, which is broader than the system itself and thus sets the stage for planning more effective political action. We begin by considering who the targets are and counting their cost.

Who Are the Targets and Potential Targets and What Is Their Cost?

The most obvious B identified are the managing partners. What was the cost to the managing partners? They had to keep people inside the organization happy because their prestige in the firm was linked to doing so. And, keeping relationships open and healthy was also a key resource for the organization. The partners relied on the managers to keep projects moving, the staff motivated and working hard, and ultimately, clients well-served.

Even though the managing partners supported the new program initially, it is important to think about the cost even to supporters for several reasons:

1. Support changes. This is a business reality. You may be perfectly well "supported" in your firm and well-liked, but support changes according to dependencies. Simply put, if a new program threatens people you support, the idea may lose.
2. Ongoing support is needed.
3. Count on resistance on other levels, making the support of this top group even more important.
4. If resistance emerges in an organized way, it is important to think about which way the top would likely go. (In this case, when real resistance organized, the partners ended up backing down from supporting the program and rallied behind their managers instead.)

Sometimes, top folks in companies support new ideas and programs because the plan may actually cost them the least. In short, it is easy to say yes and offer support because ideas often suggest no immediate cost.

In the case of Lisa and TQM, the hospital brass and board of directors supported TQM and were even willing to fling some money at it.

Figure 8.1
Tod and the Tax Managers

X = A wants an automated system implemented to gain a competitive edge.
X' = A wants to establish a good reputation within the firm.
X' = A wants advancement to partner level.

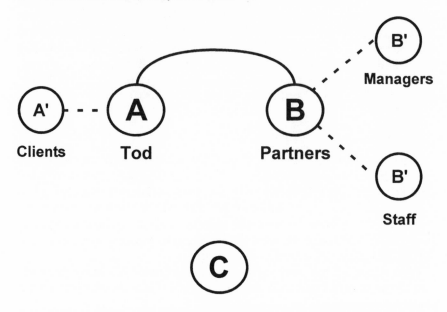

Organization Context = The firm's key dependency is client relationships.
The partners' and managers' power is derived from this hundred-year history of
doing taxes without automation.

Why? It seemed like a good idea—the competition has a program going and the top may benefit from telling the board of trustees about it.

Reality is, the top often benefits the most while paying the least cost.
That is, they aren't the ones who have to go sell the program to the
employees, do all the work to make it happen effectively while managing resistance, and yet sometimes they can reap great benefit to their
reputations for an effective new program. Simply put, the brass may well
have little to lose and much to gain from initially supporting the program. They can always attribute blame later, often to the initiator for
such reasons as inadequate data or poor implementation or planning.

All this is to say, don't ever assume that support from the top guar-
antees success. This is why we advocate counting the costs to the targets, even when "support" seems to be there for you.

Middle-Level Managers and Staff: B Primes

We've discussed the managers' cost in more detail. This was a pivotal point, because this group had a large cost and also a formidable power base in the firm. And, there was an appreciable cost to the staff, whose actual jobs were potentially at risk. Even though the risk of job loss was largely a perception rather than a reality, because the intention had been to retrain the staff, this knowledge was not fully communicated, so intent was Tod upon the more salient and valuable aspects of the automated system.

The X: What Tod Really Wanted

The ABC analysis also highlights the X. Tod wanted to implement this system, but his long-term desire was to become a partner. If he had thought about this goal, he would know that it is dependent on the partners and the existing managers thinking he is marvelous. A plan that was viewed by the other managers as harming them alienated Tod from these peers and hurt his ability to make partner.

The Solution: What Actions Should Tod Take?

The analysis of the ABCs, in concert with understanding the critical underpinnings of this firm's resource base, leads us to develop a more careful action plan. What should Tod do?

We can plan actions in almost any scenario by (1) rigorous analysis of the relationship dependencies and (2) careful consideration of the available options open to any agent. First, the situation should be analyzed according to this template:

- Do the resource analysis: Realize who has the power to either support or to demolish the implementation of this plan. Work within that reality, not within a mythical belief that having top management support will be sufficient. In this case, the power was at the lateral level, in the hands of the managers.

- Do the ABC analysis: As we have discussed, there were targets more vital than the partners. They were the tax managers. Consider other agents who may be interested in moving this plan along.

- Analyze the context: The external control of a tax-consulting firm is in the hands of clients. Tod needs to be careful because what he proposes affects the external control of this firm.

- Be clear about X: What do you want, and what do you need? In this case, Tod wanted the system and, as Lisa did, he needed his reputation and the high opinion of those who could advance him through their system. As many of us do while promoting our ideas, Tod's priorities got out of focus, and he put his ideas before his long-term career plans.

Options for Strategic Action

Having done the analysis, Tod would be set to think about a clear set of options for planning action. These involve a fairly concise set of activities and thus can be considered very clearly and in a straightforward manner. We recommend considering the full set of options and then ruling out those that are either politically innappropriate or too costly. In this case, Tod should consider the following:

- Pay the tax: Give people what they want. Determine if there is some gain to the tax managers by altering the system to take into account their interest at maintaining more discretion over client time. This is obviously a bit time consuming, but may provide reciprocal support.
- Expand the search: Look for support beyond the immediate target. This can be either with other agents or with other targets. For Tod, it is likely that he would have more success by bringing others into his plan. For example, a select few partners may be quite interested in an "ownership" stake in this idea and may be willing to introduce and build support incrementally with the other partners and some of the more senior tax managers.
- Build a coalition, either with available A primes or B primes. Building on the notion of targeting appropriate partners, Tod may well be successful sharing the plan with his own peers. The way the plan was brought to them raised their defenses. Here is a junior tax manager about to change a sacrosanct process. Regardless of its merits and top-level support, this scenario is always risky without having the appropriate coalition in place first—not last.
- Affect the context. Tod might have gathered some data on the information system he was proposing and built up the merits and time-saving value of these systems, in advance of suggesting it to his firm.
- Ignore the dependency and resolve the dilemma alone. In this case, as in most work-related situations involving interdependency, this can be disastrous. In particular, a junior person who needs lateral support to implement a plan cannot engage in this option successfully.
- Change the desire or X. Reframe the problem as discussed later.

Paying the Tax

Tod's plan must begin with the real costs in mind. Tod should develop a new game plan based on real costs to the relevant players, beginning with himself. The way he went about this plan cost him his own career plan, on which he had been working hard for five years. All the years of overtime, impossible scheduling during tax season, and hard-earned status from his tireless willingness to go the extra mile were all jeopardized by the less-than-precise planning for this "great idea."

He might consider the costs to the targets—the threat of job loss and interference with their all important client relationships. Any presentation of the automated system should consider this and include this "tax" in the framing. This would mean the system may need to be varied and include some form of personal meetings, a continuation of commitments to specific clients, and perhaps sacrifice some of the cost savings, in favor of preserving the integrity of these relationships.

Also, he might consider "paying the tax" to the staff whose worries about job loss were nontrivial. It was a mistake to discount the potential of disgruntled groups, even if they are seemingly on the lower rung of the ladder.

Look for Support beyond the Immediate Target

In this case, the partners support was taken as the ultimate blessing to propel the success of this project. As we have discussed above, support changes. The kingpins here were the lateral relationships—the tax managers, and even to an extent, the staff who would be doing much of the actual work.

Building a Coalition

In concert with expanding the search, Tod might have built a coalition with some of the partners, who could have shared in the planning of this proposed automated system. Like many "smart" managers, Tod had a personal stake in his idea, and didn't want to share the glory for this proposal. Building a coalition, with some significant others, either at the partner level or with other tax managers, and taking time to build incremental support would have been smarter than his "Lone Ranger" approach.

Affect the Context

The relevant context is that the firm has done business a certain way for a hundred years. Tod needs more than a month to present an idea and change the way this traditional firm does business, which is and has always been to have the client relationship at the center.

Ignore the Dependency and Resolve the Dilemma

For a number of reasons, this option would likely be a disaster in this situation. Tod could request funds to implement his system as a test case to demonstrate its effectiveness. However, the interdependent nature of this firm and the real need for others to support and implement his plan make this option an unlikely match for this situation. We present the option because it is one planners typically neglect, particularly when caught in a power imbalance. As we described in Chapter 2, we create our own dependencies. Tod, if he had really wanted to and didn't mind the obvious costs involved, could think about his own consultancy business, advising the consultants. This idea is a bit out of the box, but is worth a consideration.

Change the X

The final option is for Tod to reconsider how he has defined this problem. What does he really want? It is important to acknowledge that there is usually more than one defined desire in planning action. Todd wants the system and he wants his reputation to advance, but what he really wants is to make partner. Therefore, he must plan this system in a way that is consistent with all three goals, being careful not to destroy his own friendship network in the process. He should redefine what he wants and begin from there.

Once Tod is clear about his short- and long-term goals, he should assess the critical resources systematically. Understanding the firm's critical resources illuminates the dependencies. These also suggest the costs to the firm and the players—the real costs, not the monetary costs.

Only with this understanding of context can action planning begin. Next, implementation plans should include the detailed steps, which include people, relationship, resources, and cost orientations, and not just process steps.

CONCLUSION: WHAT'S A TAX MANAGER TO DO?

Tod's five years of success in this high-powered firm needn't have been demolished. He realized this himself, as he worked through his case retrospectively. Planning with his own goals more clearly defined and the context more rigorously illuminated, Tod's chief regret was that he had not "seen" the situation more clearly early on. "Why didn't I realize my own myopic viewpoint?" Tod questioned. "I just counted on the partner's support." Recall that this was a fundamental assumption for Lieutenant Tom as well. Both counted on support without counting the cost of what it would take for the tax managers or the officers to support the initiative.

This is precisely why smart people fail. Simply put, we become enamored with our own ideas and neglect the all important context within which those ideas must find support. We think of the plan when we should be thinking of the resource and dependencies of the key players who must carry our great ideas into reality. This is what happened to Tom. Tom thought he was OK and his plan was on track because he had some committed support at the top levels. This lulled him into forgetting that he needed support from those at the parallel lateral levels.

Quickly, our great ideas take over and often more support is assumed than is real. We think "great idea" when we should be counting the costs to the players whom we affect. And finally, we think naively about whose support is needed, without a rigorous analysis of the options available to us and the need for detailed tactics for carrying out those options. Overall, the support for and actual implementation of such a large change takes time, careful planning, and rigorous execution, but the result is far more likely to be success rather than failure.

9

The Case of "All the Responsibility and None of the Authority"

In the two cases of Lisa and Tod, great ideas were initiated by smart, upper-level managers. These great ideas were then thwarted by their coworkers at subordinate and lateral levels. As it became clear to their colleagues what the brilliant new philosophy and system would "cost" them, their external and internal constituents generated opposition.

In this chapter, we present one additional recurrent theme of why smart people fail. This is the theme of having all the responsibility and none of the authority needed for accomplishing one's objectives. Unlike the first two themes, wherein the actors held the authority, but none of the power; these cases demonstrate the problem of having no authority, even while given the responsibility for success.

THE CASE OF ALISON IN JAPAN

Here is the case of a young, ambitious woman in the trade marketing industry who found herself struggling for three years to accomplish ambitious responsibilities with formal, but no real authority. Alison was an American who worked for three years in trade marketing at the Tokyo branch of the British Tourist Authority (BTA). Alison's job as travel trade marketing manager was to build relationships in Tokyo and promote the BTA's advantages. She worked with a Japanese man, who we will call Yoko, the manager of consumer marketing. Both reported to Fred, the director of the entire Japanese operation.

Alison was fluent in Japanese and had lived in Japan before. She prided herself on being sensitive to Japanese cultural and business practices. She had acted as unofficial head when Fred was away, a situation which she understood had upset Yoko.

Although Alison and Yoko appeared laterally on the chain of command, Yoko had done his own job and Allison's job for fifteen years prior to her arrival. He held most of the information Alison needed to effectively do her own job in his head. There were no databases in the office. Her top-level boss was not familiar with Japanese culture and held a laissez-faire attitude concerning office politics. His style of not getting involved meant Alison needed to fend for herself in developing and expanding business contacts.

Despite the formal resources of title and experience, Alison found it very difficult to perform her job duties. The contacts in the Japanese trade knew Yoko. While it was Alison's responsibility to contact and cultivate the relationships, when Alison would call them, they in turn would return her calls and ask to deal with Yoko.

Sometimes when she and her colleagues arrived to present new ideas to clients, they would find that Yoko had already been there the day prior. When she developed new routes and tours, she would find the contacts had no resources left to purchase them because they had already purchased from Yoko. Once, she overheard Yoko describe her on the phone as someone who "unfortunately would only be at BTA Tokyo for two or three years." The implicit message was, "Don't bother working with her, she'll be leaving soon."

Eventually, Alison set up communication meetings, designed to bring Yoko onto a team and with hopes of coordinating the client work. She and her colleagues reported on their activities in these meetings, but Yoko's response typically was, "Nothing new to report." He would then take their information and use it. All the while, he did not give up his activities.

Eventually, Alison's struggle with Yoko and her inability to effectively accomplish her objectives were perceived by her superiors. They informed her that due to her difficulty managing her work relationships and inability to accomplish her responsibilities, she was being transferred. Her boss, Fred, reported that he still found her potentially quite promising and reassigned her to the London office. Her job was combined again with Yoko's, giving him what he had wanted all along.

In this situation, Alison was ineffective, with no real authority or power. This type of situation is not easily solved, and we don't mean to suggest there exists a magic bullet. However, what is unfortunate is that Alison spent three years trying to make this situation "right." She later realized her fifty-hour weeks and much effort were wasted in trying to "change" an individual while ignoring a fundamental part of the problem.

Having responsibility without authority is a redundant theme for today's managers. Many cases fill our files from clients and students faced with this dilemma. Middle-level managers find themselves in this situation quite pervasively, as do consultants. It can be frustrating if it is not well understood and managed for what it is. It is particularly confusing for managers who find themselves with all of the responsibility and none of the authority when they fail to *realize* they have no authority. Such was the case with Alison, who misdiagnosed the problem as a personality dilemma.

THE CASE OF RAY AND THE MANUFACTURING PLANT

In this next case, we develop the theme of having responsibility without authority and provide its solution. Like others, our manager Ray *thought* he held sufficient authority. This "good idea" was initiated by a powerful external governing body, and the top CEOs in the firm brought the plan to the organization. Our manager is a middle-level manager who was given the responsibility for developing the initiative. Even with external impetus and top-level support, this plan also fails when complex lateral relationships offsets it. We include it as a theme, because the theme of change failing to take place, even when it is propelled from the top, is a category within itself. We call it "all of the authority and none of the power." It involves a textbook approach to managing change (which went wrong) from a very savvy manager who worked carefully with ten different plants.

A large manufacturing company we will call XYZ planned to implement a safety program at its North American plants. The Occupational Safety and Health Administration had been applying pressures to the top management to institute a more up-to-date safety and compliance program. The company went along with this externally initiated change by putting together a team charged with designing and implementing a safety program. This team, led by our client, Ray, faced internal challenges, and the program ultimately failed, despite many factors which should have propelled its success. It had a strong, external, regulatory agency prompting the change; publicity and pressure; formidable top-level support; and careful attention to implementation detail.

The company's top executive, Jerry, initiated the new safety programs. He had dealt with OSHA concerns throughout his career and had a background in the company's minerals division as a safety-conscious manager. But, Jerry also knew what a headache getting workers to comply with the standards really was and he delegated much of the work to Joe, director of the company's North American operations. Unlike the CEO, Joe had very little experience concerning worker safety and quickly sought a responsible, up-and-coming engineer to accomplish the task. So, the CEO initiates a new safety program under pressure from OSHA. The CEO delegates to the director of operations, who delegates it to a young engineer—our client, Ray.

Ray's first task was to form a team charged with designing and implementing the project. He selected one manager from each of the North American plants with the idea of getting involvement in every stage of the process, from design to implementation and compliance. The strategy at first glance seemed like a good thing, at least from a textbook perspective. It incidentally met Joe's less public agenda, which was to delegate the task smoothly so that he himself didn't have to bother with something he viewed as less than top priority and potentially risky. Joe knew from his long experience as operations director that the guys at the plant level hated to change and found OSHA regulations a royal pain because of the interruption it caused in their production schedules.

Ray and the task team met and researched the plant manager's recommendations over the course of several months. Receiving input from a representative at each of the plants, the team designed a clear and well-detailed analysis of explicit, plant-specific problems. It also worked to provide detailed recommendations and plans for implementing those recommendations, which also were plant specific and well thought out. They presented their well-designed program, a behavior-based safety program (BBS), to both the CEO and director of operations, Joe and Jerry. The executives thought the basic principles and planned implementation sounded fine.

While the task team was busy conducting plant-specific research and preparing the report and formal presentation, the plant managers had also been busy. They learned about the proposed safety program (through the team representatives at their individual plants) and began to complain. "Why do we have to take our time to learn new safety measures when we can't get help with the old?" they argued. Some managers sent letters to the corporate executives, arguing against the proposal even before it was formally presented. "We are stretched to our limits trying to run efficient, safe, and profitable plants. And, don't forget, these safety programs require training, and so we will have to change our daily operations."

The plant managers clearly did not want yet another program that they feared would consume the resources of time and money as well as stretch them further. They also worried that they would have to deal with frustrated workers whose work routines would change and who would perceive the measure as another round of annoying management directives. The plant managers, however, couched their complaints in the rhetoric of cost. They exaggerated the potential monetary costs in their letters, but the focus worked.

Joe and Jerry understood the gist of the plant manager's concern, and they withdrew their support of the initiative, even though they had originated it. Consequently, the task team's recommendation was not accepted. Interestingly enough, the commitment not to accept the proposal was in motion and fairly well cemented, before the team even presented their proposal to the two key decision makers, Jerry and Joe, who had been the original catalysts.

Analysis: What Went Wrong Here?

The task team's failure as a group could be summarized as having several flaws. The first and most fatal flaw was that the team had subscribed to the most important myth about power. They believed that authority was the same as power. They assumed that authority from the top meant support from the bottom. They assumed that because the two top executives were promoting the change, it was as good as done.

Also, they failed to consider what the key resources and dependencies were for successful implementation. The key resource in this firm was time and production, because that is how you made money. Plant managers were rewarded almost exclusively for two things: showing profits at their plants and keeping their workers happy, without which the former could not be realized. Very simply put, the key dependencies of the plant were keeping these goals of production, time, and contented workers paramount. The new safety measures, as designed by the "guys in white shirts" directly threatened this power base.

The plan also failed to consider the key actors; rather, it believed that having initial corporate support would be adequate for success. As we saw, the real success lay with the plant managers.

Further, the plan was not context based. That is, it failed to diagnose how power is really distributed in the firm and what is most important to the firm and the people within it.

Finally, it discounted the real costs. The cost-benefit analysis only compared the cost of training for the new program against the benefit of compliance with OSHA and measurable outcomes such as decreased employee compensation time. The plan did not consider the effects of its recommendations on those who would be most essential for implementation.

This plan was a textbook design. It cost our client, Ray, his reputation at this firm because, despite the fact that the plan was initiated by the two top executives, it was assigned (or offloaded, depending on your perspective) to our client. He bore the cost of its failure from the manufacturing heads, managers, and workers, and also from the two top honchos who chose to attribute their own failure to him. Ray ended up quitting this job, which he had worked at for ten years, and going back to school for his M.B.A., in part to gain insight into how to manage people's lives more effectively.

We've discussed some of what went wrong for Ray, and we understand why he was baffled at the failure. What looked like an opportunity to propel his career up a few pegs by taking on this important responsibility and accomplishing an important goal at the direct request of the top dogs resulted in a painful exit from the firm.

It is often hard to determine who the key actors are in planning effective strategy, as they are sometimes not the most apparent or obvious. In this case, it would be reasonable to believe that Ray and the task team had the support of two corporate executives, and this would be sufficient. After all, the executives had taken the first steps for this new program and had selected the task team. However, while Ray sought approval from the executives, he lost sight of the fact that it would be the plants that would be most instrumental in whether the program was ultimately successful or not. Without their support in actually carrying out the recommendations, these recommendations were doomed. Yet, the task team focused on its plan and its implementation, virtually ignoring the real fact that in order for this plan or any plan to be ultimately successful, the individual plant manager's support would be essential.

ABC Analysis for Action Planning

A realistic ABC model could be applied to this case, which would clearly pinpoint the actors, context, and goals (see Figure 9.1). With this model in mind, the real job of the task team is clearer. The goals of Ray and the task team can be seen more clearly—this is not just about getting a safety program in place. It is about keeping the numerous plant managers happy, which in turn provides the perception of success to the chief executives, while complying with external standards. As we have noted, the real decision makers are the individual plant managers, who are as important as Joe and Jerry, because without their support, the safety program wasn't going anywhere. These individuals should be brought into the process early on to build ongoing commitment.

Further, the ABC model illustrates a clearer understanding of the X and X prime—that is, the immediate X is to have the safety program design accepted by the corporation. An equally critical X is to have the program supported by the plant managers. Finally, the X prime is the individual's goal—whether this particular safety program is initiated is less important than maintaining a credible relationship with his plant manager or his immediate boss. When individuals are ap-

Figure 9.1
Ray and the Manufacturing Company

X = A wants to gain Joe and Jerry's approval.
X' = A wants to design a safety program for all North American plants.
X' = A wants to comply with OSHA standards.
X' = A wants to retain favor at their plants.

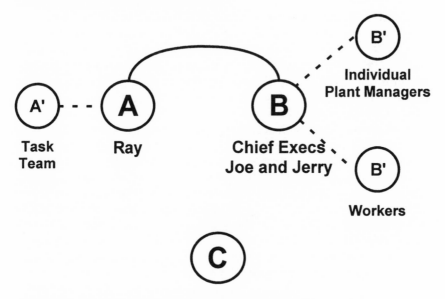

Organization Context = There are resources in competition.
Safety is not as important a criterion for advancement as performance.

pointed to, or volunteer for, corporate-level task forces or teams, the political balancing of corporate-wide interests versus local interests can be challenging. In this case, Ray scored no points with his own plant workers or his plant manager by recommending a safety program with high costs and frustrations to the local guys.

Costs to the Key Actors

Once the key actors are clearly designated, as facilitated by the ABC model, the costs to the relevant actors can be more adequately assessed. As we discussed in Chapter 6, it is important that the agent count the costs to him or herself. In this case, there was a real cost to the task team members, most of whom initially thought of their appointment as a mere honor or salute to their judgment. They could, however, raise the ire of their individual plant managers, who can in turn affect their careers. They can also be viewed as having been part of a losing effort if nothing is effected. For Ray there were also high personal costs. Somewhat blinded by the general honor of being appointed head of the committee, he neglected to consider his own costs.

The cost to the plant managers is, as we discussed above, most formidable. They need to be seen as safety compliant, but are quite aware that their individual futures don't rest with safety programs. And, if the new programs take them over their budgets or cause them to report a loss, that is data that will harm them in their standing with their own bosses.

Also, there is some cost to the executives. They don't want to upset plant managers, yet they need basic compliance measures and want something more effective than what they've got. Putting the risk for introducing this program onto the shoulders of a task team was somewhat shrewd, if borderline devious.

Now, armed with consideration of key actors and costs, what strategy should have Ray undertaken? Recognizing that the critical dependency rests with the plant managers, he should have built a coalition of support and commitment from them. Realizing that the program has relatively high costs of resources and risk to both the plant managers and the two executives, a reasonable strategy would be to test the program at just one plant to minimize the risk. The task team could request additional resources from the two executives to promote the success of a "test case." By doing so, the task team "shares the costs" of this program and also builds support from the two critical targets: the executives and the plant managers.

A plant that had a particularly bad safety record should be selected, so that incentive to adopt a program would be higher and also the results predictably more dramatic. Presumably, the plant manager would be more motivated to implement a new program and could become part of both the design and implementation. The selected plant and safety program could be highlighted in the company-wide newsletter for some public relations value. The actual success would be quite hard to measure in the initial stages, but since the plant managers were more concerned with what value the program has (in terms of its perceived importance to their bosses), public relations efforts could be quite useful at addressing this cost.

People have a way of deciding what is important by witnessing what gets rewarded in an organization. Just as organizations say they want one set of behaviors while rewarding opposite behaviors, reward systems can also be designed that facilitate new and desirable behaviors. In this case, rewarding the plant manager and the facility that showcased the new program would communicate to the other plant managers that safety-program adoption is important and valued by the executive team.

The top executives didn't want to play after they realized the plant managers might resist implementation. Once they had been able to demonstrate one successful case and had obtained the support of one plant manager, the team could have asked for additional resources. As the program became public in the organization, it would be difficult for the executives to back out of it without losing face. This is how commitment works. Having carefully demonstrated how the program was successful, the momentum is now underway for further success. The same type of modeling has a way of building widespread support.

Lessons of the Case

What lessons of this case are applicable to other arenas? This case theme repeats over and over because people are often "put in the middle" of implementing a new idea or program. Sometimes an individual or middle-level manager will be quite cognizant of the fact that what the upper echelon wants may compromise his or her own standing. As in Ray's situation, they may be given all the responsibility and none of the authority to implement a new high-risk program or change.

Recognizing this, the middle-level manager cannot ignore the political situation and should indeed plan with the political realities that are paramount to success in mind or face very real failure and potential job loss. As we have argued from the outset of this book, these types of political situations require as much rigor in planning as any other problem. The stakes are as high, if not higher.

In sum, Ray analyzed his failure in retrospect. He learned by doing the ABC analysis that the more critical target existed out of his immediate awareness. He thought about the costs to the various targets and himself. Then he planned from the set of options, including keeping his own cost in mind; building coalition; altering the X to adopt a more conservative program; and expanding the targets to bring the plant managers into the equation. While Ray analyzed his failure in hindsight, we turn next to a case wherein the analysis was done and strategic direction achieved tangible results.

To elaborate further on the case theme of having all the responsibility and none of the authority, we turn to a success case where support was needed and obtained.

KEN AND A *SUCCESSFUL* CHANGE EFFORT AT A LARGE SEMICONDUCTOR FIRM

This next case demonstrates the successful implementation of a good idea. We include it here to provide a template for managing a complex process change via the diagnosis of resources, dependencies, and the use of the ABC planning and implementation tool. In this case, Ken begins to face failure for the same reasons that Lisa and Tod failed: a less than careful appreciation for the context of his idea and an initial plan for building support that was less than rigorous. During the time Ken was attempting to introduce a change into the process of semiconductor manufacturing, he was a student in the Executive Education M.B.A. program. He worked with our template for successful implementation of an innovative idea. He was successful in a situation involving complex lateral relationships over which he had no control within a culture that was not initially supportive.

In this case Ken attempted to implement a process change involving four different units whose initial difficulties and near failure turned to success. As a young turk, Ken needed the support of the older, more experienced engineers in his firm. The change was a very small one but was complicated because Ken had very little authority over his own or the other units whose support was essential.

Ken's credentials included an Ivy League education, a newly acquired master's degree in engineering, and seven years of work experience in this firm. These credentials might be impressive on a piece of paper, but in this particular firm, the average engineer had twenty years of experience. Education meant less—far less—than experience in this firm. In fact, the older guys scoffed at the educational credentials of the younger echelon. "When we were hired," went the story, "a degree in engineering meant everything. Now, these new guys come in here with fancy Master's degrees and worse yet, M.B.A.s, and think they can tell us how to run the show. They don't know anything."

But Ken did know something and wanted to implement a process change. He was in charge of a value analysis project to identify cost savings for a new line of circuit breakers. Circuit breakers represented a $200 million a year line for this firm but were manufactured outside of the country. What Ken's six-month project revealed was that one of the parts used in the circuit breakers could be replaced with a plastic part. This would save the firm at least $5 million a year in production costs, even allowing for the initial costs, with further savings of several million to be realized within two to three years.

Several of the firm's competitors had already switched to the new plastic part, but still Ken sat down with this finding and thought about all the things that could go wrong. He consulted several other design, metallurgical, and manufacturing engineers outside his firm. Ken was sharp and asked poignant questions, even playing his own devil's advocate: "Is this change *really* a cost savings? If using plastic is such a good idea, why didn't Barry (his supervisor) think of it sooner? Is the competitor who switched to plastic having any unforeseen problems?"

Convinced that the change itself was a good one for the firm for both cost savings and production, he set about to make it happen.

Changing one small part in a manufacturing process to plastic, with such a demonstrable cost savings, should not be difficult. Ken went about it by asking himself several critical questions.

- What is the context into which the new process must fit?
- What are the critical resources and dependencies of the firm and the relevant actors?
- Who holds power? How is that power distributed?
- What external controls govern this firm?
- We diagrammed the ABCs of the political, interdependent relationships and designed an action plan, with full consideration of the nontangible costs of Ken's plan.

Assessing the Culture of the Firm

As in any change, the context is paramount, weighing far more in importance than the idea itself. As we assessed the context of this organization, Ken could readily understand that the issues that could create success or doom his plan were tied up in the culture of this one-hundred-year-old organization and its critical resources and dependencies.

No doubt, we have all worked in or interacted with businesses that have cultures, sometimes known as "dinosaur cultures"—a culture with assumptions, beliefs, values, behaviors, structures, rewards, and hierarchy based on business practices of earlier time periods. Cultures often become very strong, with practices and ways of doing business deeply entrenched and hard to change.

In this country, banking, manufacturing, and universities proliferated around the turn of the century and quite often tend to have very strong cultures. Many of the nation's most prominent companies have a hundred-year-old history and came of age at the turn of the century, a time when Taylorism was dominant. Taylorism is based on efficiency and the belief that there is one best way of doing things, in manufacturing in particular. Added to this was the administrative model of Henry Fayol. This paradigm involved a clear chain of command, a functional structure, rules, and strict hierarchical command. Such was the hundred-year-old business in which Ken worked as an engineer. In this culture, efficiency and hierarchy were valued over effectiveness.

Resources and Dependencies

Culture very much influences the way resources and dependencies are perceived and managed. What a firm believes to be important is often as vital as what truly is critical to success. The key resources of this firm were experience and the knowledge, which was assumed to reside in the engineers. Interestingly enough, this manufacturing firm had been in trouble for years, because its culture fostered the belief that it would remain strong against competition and so continued to rely on that which had stood the test of time: its engineering products, its engineers, and its time-honored traditions.

At the time of this incident, both domestic and international competition was threatening this manufacturing firm, but its managers, from the CEO down, continued to believe this threat would be short lived, as long as the firm held onto what it had "always done right." Along those lines, products and product development were considered the firm's core competency. It was known for superior products and shunned any criticism that it could no longer produce those products in a cost-effective manner relative to the competition.

"Process efficiencies are not what made this company strong," pontificated the president, "and we are not going to start fussing about penny-pinching now. We have always had and will always have superior products. We are proud of that."

Proud indeed. What Ken knew, as did a whole cadre of the younger engineers, was that their competitors were drowning them by actually producing superior products because they could achieve higher cost savings.

Who Holds Power?

It was not hard to see who holds power in the firm. The culture supported a hierarchy. People were promoted who stayed in line and did their jobs without a lot of innovative change. The older engineers had come to management positions by enforcing product focus. Power was distributed according to position in the hierarchy. And, while innovation was touted, innovation here meant ideas had strict boundaries and needed to go up the chain of command.

Planning for Change

Ken's plan was to change a small piece of the circuit breaker and replace it with plastic, while keeping his working relationships intact, because he was committed to this firm and depended on staying in one location. As we sat down to plan the change, we realized that the change involved four units. The design engineers and Ken's division manager would have to approve the change. The molding plant manager would have to support testing of the new lower-cost materials. This meant Ken would need to win support against other competing projects. Circuit breakers were actually manufactured in the firm's plant in Puerto Rico. The process change would impact this plant as well. Finally, Ken's own plant would have to change some of its quality-control measurements to test the changed circuit breaker after it was manufactured.

Here we have four units, eight managers, two off-site locations, and supervisory controls, all within a culture that is very slow to change. Yet, Ken realized that he would have to work with and not against this slow change culture and the existing hierarchy if his process change were to have any chance whatsoever.

From Culture to Costs

As we moved from analyzing the context to measuring the nontangible costs and on to examining the various actors, the costs to Ken loomed large. For Ken, trying to implement change in an organization that disdained real change could be very costly indeed. In addition, the type of change Ken proposed was of the very sort that was not part of this firm's mind-set. His was a process change, in a world where products reigned supreme. Because Ken realized that what looked like a tiny change in a piece of plastic instead was really a change involving the processes developed and enforced over a hundred years, he set out to plan rigorously and to go very slowly, as one might with any other large-scale project.

The ABC Analysis

As we reviewed the ABCs (see Figure 9.2), a few things became obvious. Ken's power for effecting this change was obviously weak in regard to numerous targets: competition from other engineers for resources and a culture that worked against his plan. For this innovation to be successfully implemented, Ken would need two things: (1) a carefully constructed plan and (2) an ally, or someone who had more clout than he, who could also promote the change.

As Ken worked through his available options, he put together a plan based on these five actions:

- Pay the tax.
- Look for support beyond the immediate target.
- Build a coalition.
- Affect the context.
- Change the X.

Paying the Tax

Ken realized that a certain tax would be required to be paid due to the culture at his business. People didn't embrace innovation simply for its own sake, but they were interested in an innovation only if it fit

Figure 9.2
Ken at the Electronics Firm

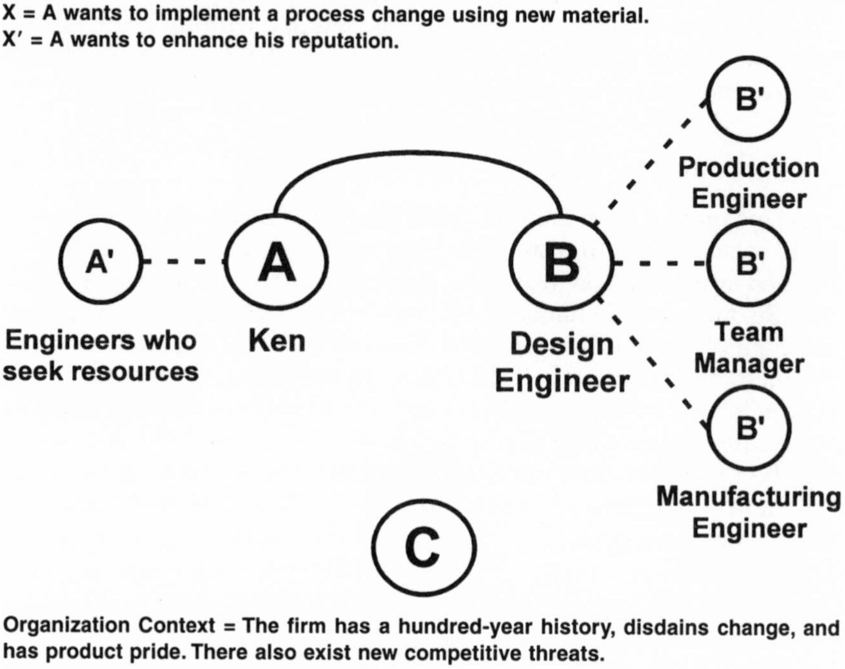
X = A wants to implement a process change using new material.
X′ = A wants to enhance his reputation.
A'
Engineers who seek resources
A
Ken
B
Design Engineer
B'
Production Engineer
B'
Team Manager
B'
Manufacturing Engineer
C
Organization Context = The firm has a hundred-year history, disdains change, and has product pride. There also exist new competitive threats.

within existing values, such as creating superior products. Moreover, in this culture, people who brought forth their ideas as "Lone Rangers" seldom lasted very long. Ken shaped the idea within this context and set out to illustrate how his idea would improve products.

Seek Support beyond the Immediate Target

Most assuredly, Ken would need support beyond an immediate supervisor since his plan involved numerous other departments. The dependency analysis illustrated Ken's weak position. He would need an ally. Also, within this culture, any change originating from someone with less than ten years of in-house experience was doubly suspect.

Unfortunately, his sole potential ally in the design department was his boss. She was viewed as a competitor at the outset because she too wanted to make a change that would involve the resources of the testing facility and the manufacturing plant. Ken's plan would likely be perceived as competing for those same resources.

Ken thought of how he could bring this potential ally to his side of the equation and make her an ally rather than competitor. Ken saw how his proposal could enhance her own proposal, which emphasized higher performance for the circuit breakers. She was seeking an engineering improvement in the circuit breakers by using higher performance molding. Ken saw some similarities—both would involve an identical testing sequence and approval from the same individuals. This could involve competition; but Ken presented it as synergy.

Build a Coalition of Support

Ken presented his plan to his boss, Karen, as one which would meet her interests with reciprocal interests and as one which could tie the two projects together. He volunteered to do some of Karen's work—that of preparing samples for testing. By tying the two projects together, Ken built an ally and also fostered commitment for his own change. His interaction with his boss in design engineering increased. This led to Karen sharing one of her key contacts in the off-site testing facility and the change turning from "her" to "our" project. Karen was a valued design engineer and held clout with other divisions, which was significant.

The facility in Puerto Rico represented a second critical target, as outlined in the ABC model. There were significant costs involved for the molding-facility manager. Most significantly, the costs were in the risk: If the plastic did not hold up, time would be lost in production and the molding-facility manager would be blamed. A change in process changed the way his facility operated. So the question was how to obtain support for a project that represents significant costs to a target while offsetting significant competition for scarce resources.

Again, Ken moved to build a coalition. As he found a reciprocal support through Karen, he was able to obtain more resources to support the project. The first was time. By getting some time off, he was able to spend time in the Puerto Rican facility, offering to perform the testing under the supervision of the molding-facility manager. He tested Karen's project at the same time. Ken also did some other work in the plant during his down time. The project then became less "Ken's project," because clearly others now held a stake in it, via their work and commitment.

Affect the Context

As a relatively young engineer, forcing change by pushing levers within the context was a difficult option for Ken. However, after building some coalition with his boss who held more clout, the two together sought to affect the context, as they targeted the off-site plants and divisions. This firm had gone on record in its more recent strategic plan and mission statement formation as saying that they sought integration among the plants to offset a sense of "separate fiefdoms." Ken and Karen both sought to make this more salient by building support among the various plant engineers.

Change the X

As we've described in other cases, people who seek to initiate and build support for change by personalizing the project, becoming focused on it as "their" project, have less success at building support. Effective innovations almost always involve a team of support. In this case, Ken needed support from twelve principles. So, it was critical for Ken to present what he wanted—his X—with the needs of these individuals in mind. As we said previously, no one in this firm liked a "hot shot," defined here as just about anyone with less than ten to fifteen years experience and who wanted to change things. Ken held this important reality in mind and was clear in both planning and actions that he wasn't seeking the glory alone for this. He shared his glory and he gained support.

Do a Behavioral Analysis

The successful implementation of this change lent itself to a behavioral analysis, as we described in Chapter 6. It is not sufficient to "need support" or even to know whose support one needs. This type of implementation, involving four interdependent units over whom the agent did not have direct control, required a careful assessment of precisely what was needed from each player and what actions each player must take.

As we discussed, a behavioral analysis begins with the X in mind. In our model, this is what the agent wants. It then works backward to determine what actions each player should take for the successful implementation of the X. In this case, the X was twofold: to implement the cost-saving process, and to preserve Ken's reputation and good standing with his senior colleagues.

LESSONS LEARNED

Ray's failure in implementing a safety program and Ken's success had much to do with their management of the political situations. In both cases, the actors needed to pay careful attention to the ABCs of the political relationship and the realities of the context, cost, and dependencies. In sum, both Ray and Ken needed to

- Do the resource dependency analysis. This gets at the critical question of who has the power. This is the reality to work within.
- Do the analysis of the larger context, and work with the resistance.
- Diagram the relationship to "see" the targets more precisely in context and to determine what levers may be pushed.

- Be clear about what your request "costs" others, and plan with their perspective in mind. What seems simple is seldom simple. Every charge costs something to somebody.

- Be very clear and thoughtful about what exactly you want and what it will cost you. Define the X to be mindful of long-term and short-term interests.

- Go through the list of available actions available to all agents in a political relationship, as we have defined.

- Choose the option and combination of options that works given the analysis above. Political action is not cheap or simple. It often involves a complexity and multiplicity of actions.

In these cases of failure and success, there are several important comparisons. We can see that Ray went straight to the final step. He planned action with great attention to detail. That model comes straight from a current business school textbook. We think the model of defining a problem, developing action planning, and executing a plan is a model that often gets people into trouble. In Ray's case, the problem he was trying to address was defined by an outside agency: OSHA's regulations. The plan was decided by his superiors; the actions were put into place with energy and vigor. The actions, however, failed to consider the interests and dependencies of the key players. His planning went straight to execution, with a nod to involving some plant-level managers, but side-stepping critical interests and critical players. This is frequently a problem. "Charging ahead" while ignoring middle-level players or the very players who have to live with and execute the plan has thwarted many managers from being successful with good ideas.

Step back from the problem-definition and action-planning approach. Instead, begin with the resource and dependency analysis. Consider our success case. Ken's plan began with the resource and dependency analysis and proceeded to consider the needs of the relevant array of targets. What resources did Ken bring to the situation? He brought not only his good idea, but offered the resource of time, involvement, and insight to one of his superiors to move her project along as well. His actions were careful and deliberate, and his plan included detailed step-by-step action planning—something very difficult to do within the tasks and emotional involvement of trying to be successful in the face of predictable resistance.

We have discussed several scenarios involving middle-level managers. Tod in tax management, Ray in manufacturing, and Ken as the youngest and least tenured of the three exhibit significant differences and contrasts in managing lateral relationships. All three desired to implement a complex innovation through many divisions, involving complex layers of managerial and employee "buy in."

Interestingly, both Tod at the tax-consulting firm and Ray as a manufacturing manager had more initial support from the top executives than did Ken, but failed to plan with rigorous attention to real costs, to fully appreciate the costs of his new plan, and to execute the plan with precision. These men were middle-level managers. Both were highly educated with excellent people skills, but one "dropped out," and one remained and moved forward in his company with respectable accolades. Ken, whose innovation involved similar complexity, was the most successful, however, because of his careful attention to lateral relationships and exacting analysis of relevant context variables. We believe the type of planning Ken engaged in and executed underscores the critical contribution of our model and stands in marked contrast to the type of general "push" strategy often advocated by management gurus. Details matter—in engineering and in people managing.

All these cases raise questions and issues about the difficulty of exacting innovation. So far, the cases we have highlighted have repetitive motifs—scenarios of smart managers trying to accomplish objectives within the context of networks of lateral relationships.

Our next set of cases address the issue of managing lateral relationships from the opposite side. What happens when people who have support and promising career trajectories get stymied not by their own plans, but by the objectives of others? And, how can we better manage when those at either lateral levels or our superiors direct actions that are definitely not in our interest? We look at numerous cases from the perspective of very accomplished individuals, ranging from a group of vice presidents, a telecommunications executive, and an accomplished project engineer, and we work through the case of an up-and-coming, M.B.A.-trained, international investment banker. All of these individuals faced challenges commonly dubbed the "abusive boss" situation.

10

The Case of "Power Shifting While You Weren't Looking"

People sometimes ask us if power abuse is avoidable. Don't individuals just routinely abuse their power? If you are stuck working for the creep, that is just life, isn't it? There is not much you can do about it, except quit. And quitting sometimes means facing an equally intractable situation, because difficult and even abusive bosses are unfortunately too commonplace. They are even the stuff of comic strips. It is no coincidence that strips such as *Beetle Bailey, Blondie*, and more recently, *The Born Loser* and *Dilbert* are quite popular—everyone relates to the clueless or abusive boss.

We believe that what many dub "abuse," however, is really a basic lack of understanding of political situations. Second, when people are in truly abusive boss situations, we don't see self-help and influence techniques (many of them quite valid, reasonable, and worth knowing in other circumstances) as sufficient. Our intention here is not to rehearse the behavior people can engage to learn to manage difficult people more effectively, because others have written about it quite well. Rather, we seek to address some very commonplace problems that are sometimes labeled "abusive." We think this labeling is far too simple and implies either a passive acceptance, on the one hand, and avoidance or confrontational style on the other. None of these behaviors is typically effective. It is usually not enough to be charming, smart, hard-working, or influential. Sometimes, the best laid influence tactics fail because of the larger context of power imbalance and the realities of political dependencies.

In this chapter, we work through the redundant theme of "abusive bosses," in situations brought to us by dozens of M.B.A. students and clients. The cases we recount present the motif of abuse in individual and situational contexts of people working diligently for difficult bosses. When people first attempt to analyze their situations, the overwhelming tendency is to simply blame the incorrigible boss, vent their frustrations, and try harder, or, conversely, to quit. As we work through these cases of the unyielding or abusive boss, we provide a different lens for analyzing these situations and fresh options for directing behavior more effectively.

One aspect of the abusive boss theme that is particularly disturbing is that people at all levels face seemingly intractable bosses. We would like to reassure readers, clients, and students in particular that education and position are sometimes, but not always, a good defense against difficult bosses. As we all know, the bad news is, the higher up you go on the organizational or corporate ladder, the pervasiveness of "abusive bosses" does not diminish, but is instead all the more perplexing. And, sometimes "abusive bosses" are integral to abusive systems, where it seems that you can't win. Perhaps most frustrating of all is the boss who generally favors and supports everyone, but turns cold toward you or even turns aggressively against you when organizational dynamics change.

So, yes, there are truly unyielding and abusive bosses. But more often, what people define as an "abusive boss" is misdiagnosed. It is important to differentiate complex politics from difficult people. There are three major mistakes people make in defining abusive bosses:

1. Abuse usually has more to do with political situations than individuals.
2. Abuse is often misattributed to being in a losing division or assigned a losing project.
3. Abuse is often misattributed because power shifts and the boss no longer has the resources promised.

In our first vignette, we illustrate what many would define as a truly abusive boss who generates insecurity. Our client, a vice president at the firm, worked out a simple solution to manage his own political situation during the period. The second vignette illustrates the first of the errors and demonstrates how to manage politics that masquerade as abusive bosses. We discuss the case of a telecommunications worker taking a position on the eve of a major restructuring. The third concerns a smart project engineer who happened to be assigned unwittingly to a failing product. In this case, the boss simply could not deliver what had been promised and intended in different circumstances. The remainder of the chapter is devoted to presenting a detailed, tactical solution to the dilemma of managing the "abusive" boss when the real problem is situational. We call this motif, "The case of power shifted and you weren't looking."

THE CASE OF THE ABUSIVE CEO AND
THE VICE PRESIDENTS

One client reports a case well suited to the definition of abusive boss. A particularly insecure and nasty man was at the helm of a large manufacturing plant. His habit at monthly executive meetings was to call his vice presidents or middle-level managers on the carpet for problems within their divisions. This embarrassed the managers sufficiently before their colleagues and it bred a perverse sort of loyalty to the CEO's whims and directives. It also fostered a nervous anxiety among the managers, which they in turn passed on to their own workers to exact standards and constantly higher taxes in the form of sheer hard work.

This CEO had another habit which kept his VPs on their toes (and on everyone else's). He routinely took problems in a division to the vice president's direct reports, attributing blame by suggesting that the "real" issues were the fault of the middle-level managers. This served to infuriate his middle managers, who both wanted and needed the goodwill and respect of their own people. Yet, as is not surprisingly the case, these ten vice presidents feared to cross the chief honcho. Over time, the situation deteriorated, as fear and anxiety replaced any semblance of open communication with the chief. Added to this was an uncertainty, partly fostered by the CEO, that certain divisions were going to become dispensable in the next few years. Purposefully creating competition among his vice presidents served to generate a climate of distrust among the VPs.

Two of the VPs decided to take the direct approach and requested meetings with the CEO to discuss the detrimental affect of these fear tactics. As you may have guessed, both of these VPs witnessed a retaliation. Although they were not directly fired, they experienced cuts in their budgets and staffing and an even sharper critique of their performances, leading one to quit and the other to be quiet about problems.

Our client (after filling his fifth prescription for medication to manage the pervasive anxiety) was determined to take the risk of seeking support among the other VPs. He set up quiet meetings, at first with one of his trusted colleagues, and finally with all but two of the other VPs. They formed a corporate support group, meeting biweekly. By sharing notes, support, and real information, they found an unusual type of collective action. The group realized that they could neither confront the CEO nor the board of trustees and rightly guessed that any information taken to the board would work against them. As long as the guy was making money, the board was happy. There was not a lot of political action to take, since they were truly outranked in power.

Nevertheless, this group of VPs found the support among their colleagues diminished their emotional dependency upon the CEO. They were better able to manage Monday morning outbursts and individual critiques, knowing they had the inner, if not the momentary verbal, support of their colleagues. And, through their information sharing, they came to know that the boss's years were likely to be numbered. Survival by outlasting the CEO and the provision of tangible support from fellow colleagues became the successful game these VPs learned. Better yet, they developed some collective capability to reframe problems and present them as a whole, making it more difficult for the ruthless CEO to target and devour individuals.

MARY AND THE TELECOMMUNICATIONS FIRM

Mary was a rising-star technical manager at a telephone company. She faced an all too common situation and what some might deem a losing situation. Mary had accepted a position at a burgeoning telecommunications company. She had been an executive at a smaller telecommunications firm and was hired by the larger firm for her stellar reputation with problem solving and "turn around" solutions. Mary was lured by promises of even higher levels of management, and gave up her security and successful reputation at a smaller telecommunications firm for the promise of new levels of responsibility. What she did not realize at the time she was signing on with this firm was that the firm was embarking on great change.

The CEO was replaced shortly after Mary's hire, and the new CEO preached integrative, team-oriented management. Great stuff. It also meant almost complete restructuring in a manner that did not suit Mary's original hopes. The position she had been promised evaporated in the restructuring. As is common with restructuring, during a time of great change, there are likely to be not one but multiple reorganizations. When the first reorganization occurred, Mary bit her lip and stayed low. She focused on the work she had been assigned, even though it seemed beneath both her level and expectations. Within the next year, Mary kept her ears open and realized that her division was on insecure footing with the next pending wave of restructuring. Not only was Mary's promised position gone, but her work within her division was likely to be in vain as well.

Before the second restructuring occurred, Mary requested an audience with the supervising vice president in charge of the reorganization. Mary made it clear that the Los Angeles market, for which she had been originally responsible, represented almost half of the total capital budget, amounting to over $1 billion of spending. She proposed a plan to the vice president that this market required special action, as it should be split apart from the other markets the company served. Simultaneously, a crisis occurred in the Los Angeles market that caught the attention of the division president. "Why was this not foreseen?" the president asked. Mary stepped in quickly and resolved the crisis. In the third reorganization, Mary was named as the head of the specialized Los Angeles market.

This case has a fortunate ending—a manager was politically aware in the wake of a political disaster. She realized where the critical needs were of her firm. Had Mary been less knowledgeable or forthcoming, it is likely she would have been a victim rather than a hero. This experience had more to do with the firm's situation than with the individual CEO, but many people end up misattributing these types of frustrating situations to personal bosses. They can't win, because the problem is not the boss, but the political situation. Until that is realized, no amount of charm, bargaining, or negotiating is likely to be effective. Neither is getting angry, frustrated, or passive likely to get you anywhere.

There are two quick strategies for managing abusive bosses or potentially abusive situations. In the first example, a group of VPs avoided the direct confrontational route and found support via a political network, keeping their own career trajectories intact while waiting out the CEO's demise. In the second example, Mary changed a dependent situation from passive reactance to a success by keeping in tune with the critical needs of the firm and eventually affecting her boss's perception of the situation. These two vignettes represent the simpler and clearer issues of abusive bosses or potentially malevolent situations. Nevertheless, if not managed, these frequently spell career suicide.

In our next set of cases, we take a vigilant look at several very difficult situations to demonstrate the fundamental principle of this book: how to work successfully with the intractable. The accomplished men in the longer case vignettes that follow faced obstinate work situations. We discuss these cases in detail because managing abusive bosses and the intractable contexts in which one finds them will be one of the most truly relevant challenges of the twenty-first century work place.

In both the case of John, a project engineer, and Roberto, a highly successful investment banker, personality, charm, and hard work were insufficient to manage their situations. The cases demonstrate that what is often labeled "power abuse" often has more to do with individuals failing to understand the underpinnings of power in lateral relationships. Both accomplished men experienced power shifts that affected their critical internal relationships and caused both individuals to plummet into career infernos. We believe they represent a common problem paradigm and provide a template for managing these types of scenarios.

BEING ASSIGNED THE LOSING HORSE
(AND NOT KNOWING IT)

This scenario represents the common situation of being assigned a project that is a risk or even a lemon—yet, there you are, put in charge of it. We dub this type of situation "the case of being assigned the losing horse (and not knowing it)."

John was a moderately successful project engineer working on the West Coast at a time when automated teller machines (ATM) were coming into vogue. The bank he worked for had reviewed proposals from numerous ATM vendors, each claiming to have the best technology, and the bank was about to begin testing four of the competing vendors. John's responsibility was to serve as liaison between the vendor and the bank. His job was to test how the vendor's ATM products would work with the existing banking network.

John's boss had assigned each of the four competing vendors to individual project managers. John had three months to oversee internal research, external market research, and to test the vendor's product with the bank's needs. He would then give his boss an analysis from which to make a selection decision among the competing vendors. The bank had suffered in the past by being dependent on machines manufactured by one vendor who stopped providing upgraded models. To avoid the problem of over dependence on one vendor, the bank was looking to integrate two new vendors and wanted the very best product available corresponding to their technical demands and customer friendly mission.

Both the bank and the vendors had a great deal of money riding on the project. For the vendors, the opportunity to have their ATM machines at roughly forty thousand banks represented about a $20 million project. For the bank, having the best ATM vendors was critical. For John, being part of this critical project and decision process represented a promotion, and so he began his task ambitiously.

John's job involved coordination between the vendor and the various supporting technical departments of the bank who would perform the testing and system design. This meant setting up time and testing resources with the information-systems personnel, including the programmers, integration testers, and librarians who managed the computer program to run the ATMs. And, it involved obtaining testing resources from the market-research team. As John set out, he realized that while the project engineers were John's colleagues and were all employees of the same bank, there was an unspoken competition among them, as each identified with his own particular representative vendor. John soon found that he was not able to get cooperation from the people he was depending on for testing and information. They typically cited overwork or business for one of the other project engineers as reasons why testing John's work fell behind.

Although John kept his boss abreast of the difficulty he was having in obtaining time and resources, he was not in a position to directly lobby for the needed resources. Further, the managers met weekly to assess the progress of their engineers and the vendors—however, the project engineers were not included in these meetings. John had to rely on his boss to voice his requests. He assumed that by keeping his boss informed that he was having cooperation problems, he had his boss's understanding for the delay. By the third month, and with this assumption, John went ahead and took a scheduled two-week vacation. When he returned, he found his project had been put on hold with someone else assigned to facilitate.

Unbeknownst to John, his boss had already selected a favored vendor, and John's vendor was in competition with that choice. Also, the other project engineers had banded together to obtain their testing time and needed resources and had made John and his vendor look incompetent by contrast. What began as a promotion ended in real humiliation for John. He relayed this situation to us as an M.B.A. student about two years after it had happened. It had left a lasting impression on him, and he had internalized the problem as the result of his own incompetence. He felt humiliated after that incident and ended up leaving the firm a few months later.

Fundamental to this problem was the political context. The boss had a favored vendor. The other project engineers were competitors for resources in this scenario, and John's project was not going to "win." What's important in the scenario of being assigned the losing project is to recognize it as such and to work within that context. In this context, to "win" would mean to ascertain what the boss really wanted. Instead, John identified with the vendors and got caught up in a competition for resources with his colleagues, harming some relationships in the process. If John had first assessed his own costs and his own dependencies, he would have recognized that maintaining reputation and favor with his boss was more important than fighting for resources with his colleagues. Being assigned the losing project by a boss who doesn't level with you is only a no-win situation if you don't understand the game.

Why Do Bosses Play Games?

This question may be best left to ethicists. The fact is they do, and your job is to understand the game and win. We would define winning in cases like John's, to start by understanding that he had been assigned to a losing project. There may have been a good, or at least valid, reason why his boss had to entertain four vendors for testing and review. One plausible reason is that four options meant the vendors developed a competition that might serve the bank's interests very well. Or by demonstrating to his higher-ups that he had tested four vendors and selected one, John's boss may be viewed as having made a more credible and justifiable decision. Decision makers routinely engage in this strategy. For example, this is the game played when a search is conducted for a position but the decision makers know full well that an internal candidate has the job in the bag. Sometimes this is for legal purposes, but more often than not having options fosters both power and credibility. So understanding the game of being assigned the losing project is the first task.

Second, sometimes people and their projects get set up to fail for other, more insidious reasons. The minority or lone female in a division, for example, may be intended for failure. An important key is reading the power, as we have discussed earlier in this book. It is critical, even for new hires, to know if they have been assigned to a losing division, or just where their group, department, or project stands in the overall power network. If this is the case, early recognition is critical to avoid overinvesting resources of time, talent, career, or loyalties to the internal environment.

THE CASE OF POWER SHIFTING WHILE YOU'RE NOT LOOKING: ROBERTO AND INTERNATIONAL BANKING

Another form of the abusive boss case and what is often labeled as unfair behavior is when an individual is very dependent on one boss. This is competition of a different nature. We find this type of scenario occurring with increasing frequency as organizations go through structural changes.

Sometimes, people do everything right in their organizations. They do more than a good job—they do a splendid job. They manage their way into positions of authority and power in the right sections of organizations. On top of that, they learn how to manage their important relationships with great élan. They manage relationships outside of their immediate departments well and learn how to acquire increasing resources and perform a valuable role within the interdepartmental complex network.

Such was the situation for Roberto in the complex, fast-paced world of international banking. Classified as brilliant, Roberto was educated at top-notch schools and aced the finance program at an Ivy League university. To his boss, he was a valuable resource not merely for his financial acumen, but for his multilingual fluency in building relationships with a variety of customers and contacts with other divisions. This very reliance also was the source of some abuse by his boss.

Roberto felt he had a good relationship with his superiors: He was well paid with frequent bonuses; highly regarded as a young player; shielded from unpleasant assignments; and assured of continued promotion for his hard work and for being "one of the insiders"—one who knew how to play the game and play it well.

But Roberto wasn't content with this status; his own capabilities and ambition almost assured him that he would seek promotion. After eight productive years in the division, with incremental promotions, Roberto surprised his boss by discussing a transfer to another division, one which Roberto had astutely realized was the up-and-coming unit. It was a move Roberto realized would be important for his long-term career goal of achieving one of the upper-management positions.

Roberto was a little surprised when his boss turned down his request. "Roberto," he said, "I realize and appreciate your ambition, son. It is what I want for you, too. We're grooming you for a top spot, but with the wave of acquisitions, here is the place to be." With that, the boss laid out a career plan, the central element of which was a promised promotion into the top divisional spot within two years. With a hefty raise, Roberto found the arrangement sound and continued to work hard. "Hard" translated to sixty-hour weeks, pursuing and managing new accounts, and as always, continuing to assist the boss with international relationships.

Roberto was working so hard, he hardly noticed it when his division was restructured. And, he barely registered that his boss had a new title. Roberto found his boss a bit short at Roberto's annual review meeting. He gave very little feedback about specific accounts and just told him keep up the good work and "of course, we'll be considering you for promotion next year." The next year, the boss was traveling with increasing frequency. Still, he assured Roberto that his coveted position would be forthcoming. At the end of this second year, the boss had been transferred to a new division as part of restructuring. As it turned out, the restructuring plans had been in the works for several years, but had not been known to Roberto, whose travel and appointments at satellite banks kept him out of the office much of the time.

What about the coveted promotion? As you may have guessed with greater ease than Roberto did, the boss was not in a position to award the promotion and hadn't been for some time. When Roberto requested a meeting to discuss the promotion with his new boss, the boss appeared taken aback. "That would be entirely out of the question, Roberto. You've done a nice job here, but we would need someone with a different background for the top spot. Actually, we've had our eye on Amad for the past few years and promised him the position. We thought you knew." Roberto left the organization shortly after that time. His initial anger turned to a deep sense of betrayal and then self-doubt, wondering all the while what he had missed.

Case Analysis

Sometimes, people do everything right in their organizations—everything except realizing that the power shifted while they weren't looking. In this case and an unfortunate large number of others we have seen, power shifted, and individuals fail to realize that the person or persons upon whom they depended were no longer able to provide the desired resource: the promotion, the raise, or sometimes even the continuation of their position.

Why does this happen? As individuals in organizations, we can't avoid the reality that power shifts. As we have discussed, power is dynamic and externally controlled, and it changes. Individuals cannot hope to avoid the manifestations of power shifts. It happens all the time. What we *can* do, however, is learn to predict the adverse outcomes of power shifts upon our personal lives and careers and learn how to manage this type of scenario more effectively.

In this case, Roberto, like most of us, was committed to a set of players—his immediate supervisors and trusted mentors. We work. We trust. We believe. We depend. Meritous qualities, all. It is normal for individuals to be committed to their goals and to those individuals who promise the achievement of those goals. In fact, most management gurus would tell you that the mentoring relationship in a firm is one of the key ingredients to an individual's success. And so it is. We advocate mentoring and the dual-sided commitment that is fostered by strong, solid relationships with individuals, particularly individuals who hold resources in organizations. It is worth looking at critically, however, when the commitment has a life of its own and becomes stronger than the reality. This blinds us to the perils of mentoring, which is that power shifts and often when it does, it affects your mentor's power. This translates quite pragmatically to the fact that your mentor of today may not be able to provide the resources you covet tomorrow. This has nothing to do with personal interest. It has to do with power and its dynamic nature and how it affects internal lateral relationships.

People who work in government accept this routinely as part of the game. When your guy is out of power in Washington, all the Republicans (or Democrats, depending on the season) go job hunting. In business organizations, a similar political landscape exists. But we are just not used to thinking of organizations as political and are often quite shocked and taken aback when our allies shift their alignment.

When realities shift, as they did in the banking industry in Roberto's case, the acquisition caused his boss's power base to change. His boss worried about his own position, even while he needed Roberto to continue to be productive to offset his own threatened reputation.

Lessons of the Case Theme

We include this case not merely to comment fatalistically upon a repetitive organizational reality. We believe this type of organizational problem can be managed more effectively by proactive assessment. Consideration of one's power base and the lateral relationships and realities that govern it is not only for a crisis or for planning specific actions. It is for everyday survival in today's complex organizations. We advocate that budding recruits, new hires, and well-tenured employees, as well as seasoned CEOs, conduct assessments of their organizations routinely. The template to follow is as follows:

- Develop a resource and dependency analysis of the industry.
- Consider the internal and external contexts of the industry, including the external control of power and internal power distribution.
- Analyze the ABCs of lateral relationships, including a clear assessment of the various targets who affect you and a clear sense of alternative agents who may be in alignment or in competition with what you want.
- Clearly consider short-term and long-term goals and how to be effective in obtaining them. Also evaluate on an ongoing basis the critical relationships and the factors that may change them.

What Could Have Been Done in Roberto's Case?

We have described how power is a product of resources and dependencies, rather than individual characteristics. In this situation, the boss's dependencies changed and his resource base changed. Roberto was looking at the individuals rather than at the organizational realities. What could he have (and what could others do) differently to avoid this type of problem?

- Read the power. Realize power is a dynamic, not a stationary, phenomenon. It isn't in the hands of individuals as much as it is a product of an organizational resource base. And so, power changes.
- Any time an organization undergoes change, in restructuring or even in changing the cast of characters, it is important to reassess the organizational power. Where are you now in this schema? How does this affect your resources? How does it affect those upon whom you depend? Such questions are not for the paranoid, but for the realistic.
- Realize that allies, even trusted ones, change. Allies change as resources and dependencies change. What are your boss's dependencies? Have they changed? Has the boss's resource base changed?
- Avoid a pigeon-hole vision of relationships. Never trust one individual to carry your reputation. The knowledge of Roberto's many, many years of

hard work and achievement were largely held by only a few individuals. As managers and individuals were reassigned, the knowledge disseminated. As the boss's prominence declined and his credibility along with it, so did the knowledge of Roberto's excellent reputation.

- Finally, Roberto could and should have moved to spend time building new relationships and with the new cast of players. He could have expanded his relationship base in the organization and thereby been more assured his reputation (his most critical resource) was not just in the hands of one player. Instead, he was living out yesterday's promises, and while his nose was to the grindstone, he found those promises dispersed to new actors in the organizational drama.

CONCLUSION

All the individuals discussed in this chapter were smart, hard-working, and accomplished in their fields. No novices here. A vice president, an M.B.A.-trained manager in telecommunications, a project engineer, and an accomplished international-banking professional represent a sample of the cases we have worked with demonstrating potentially abusive bosses. What they hold in common was a reliance upon individuals who were not up front and straightforward. But this is not uncommon. We would not label the bosses "abusive" or personally vindictive. Rather, in all of the cases, the individuals were dependent upon an individual or a system that did not have their interests in mind. Again, not an uncommon situation. But, as we have demonstrated, these situations are often career infernos. While Mary saw her way out of a potentially disastrous political situation and the vice presidents adapted by networking together, John and Roberto were significantly harmed and their careers were put into jeopardy by their own inability to manage the complex political context. We offer our analysis and planning, not as a sure-fire shield from difficult bosses and political quagmires, but to demonstrate that people needn't be victims of power abuse. We also hope to illustrate how people can avoid contributing to their own demise.

To flip these scenarios, we turn next to several cases of power at the top. As we have seen, sometimes it's the top level that manipulates power and sends people like Mary, John, and Roberto into a spin. Power at the top however is not an easy thing to manage, and those who get there very often have painfully short-lived tenure.

11

The Case of "Failure and Success at the Top"

We have presented some of the themes that circumvent smart ideas from several perspectives. Middle-level managers such as David in Chapter 7 and Ken in Chapter 9, repectively, faced difficulties despite support from their superiors when they failed to appreciate the strength of interests at lateral levels. Even upper-level managers such as Lisa the Chief Operating Officer, are faced with surprises that circumvented their work, as they mistakenly failed to identify relevant lateral relationships and the dependencies that sustain them.

Some managers believe that higher positions obviate the need for building support because authority of the position provides the needed leverage. Many a manager aspires to a higher position with such motivation. Nevertheless, as anyone who has managed from the top can attest, position and all its privileges does not negate or even reduce the need to build support and influence at lateral levels. Indeed, this is a classic myth of management. And, the stakes are higher when you lose.

Even boards of directors and CEOs must manage lateral relationships. The myth that authority is sufficient to be effective is one of the main reasons why the average CEO tenure in the United States is only about three to five years, depending on the industry. And, this myth is why so many people have a hard time holding onto power at any managerial level once they have it. Being at the top and remaining there is not a matter of pushing buttons or sending down orders. Those who study CEO failure systematically report that the failure to transfer from middle- to upper-level management is largely a product of inability to manage relationships. But what does that mean in concrete terms? We hold that effective management of relationships at the top is not about interpersonal skills or charm, charisma or coercion, manipulation or Machievellianism. It begins with astute understanding of the lateral relationships, which in the case of CEOs, an even more complex context, which can either make or unravel the best-laid plans.

In the following cases concerning the CEO role, we see how the chiefs either worked with or against the important lateral relationships and consequently failed or succeeded in very complex worlds. We include these cases to demonstrate the critical role of dependencies and resources even at the top level and to support our argument that authority doesn't necessarily make it easier to get things done.

In the next two situations of CEO-level management, we take a broader look at this type of problem and demonstrate a strategy for thinking about and managing these types of lateral relationships more effectively. The first case concerns a case of short-lived power and eventual failure at managing lateral relationships from the CEO level; the second is about a successful CEO.

THE CASE OF THE UNIVERSITY:
THE RISE AND FALL FROM POWER, OR HOW POWER IS
LOST ONCE YOU'VE GOT IT

When the new president (we will call him John) at a "big city" university took over leadership, he was welcomed with accolades. Great expectations accompanied the arrival of this new president and the front page of the city newspaper carried this headline: "The New President of the University Welcomed with Open Arms." And, indeed he was snugly welcomed by both the internal community at the university— faculty, staff, and students—and by the very critical local business community. A little more than three years later, the same newspaper proclaimed the following terse and yet revealing two-word headline: "(John): Out."

What happened in this short three-and-a-half year span that caused the competent Dr. John, to be at first welcomed with accolades and then rejected with embarrassment? This is a case of the rise and fall from power of a very competent leader. It is also a scenario that repeats all too often in American business.

Rising to a top position is not for the faint of heart or the grossly incompetent. People spend a lifetime of hard work, sacrifice, and perseverance to achieve top-status levels. Why then do accomplished people have such a difficult time managing and maintaining top positions once they achieve them? Let's consider this case, for it reveals a common theme about losing power.

Background and Context

This situation takes place in a university context. There are complicated internal and external environments (and fuzzy borders between the two). Its members retain a stakeholder role via alumni relationships. There are thousands of alumni in the general city area, many of whom now form the backbone of the local business and political communities, including local politicians, judges, CEOs, and managers of health-care organizations. Concerning internal workings, the university is the second largest employer in the city. It has diverse departments with unique cultures, ranging from drama to top-ranked engineering, medical, and law schools—all of which sprawl across an urban campus. The university president reports to a board of trustees, many of whom are former alumni and all of whom are top-level executives in a number of regional and national organizations. Many of these organizations also have a stake in the university.

The external environment is similarly complex with numerous academic competitors, a dynamic, fast-paced medical environment, and a resource base involving substantial revenue from alumni and about one-third of the operating budget from state sources. In addition, the university is moderately unique, in that more than 50 percent of its hundreds of thousands of alumni reside in the area. This provides a very strong locus of external control, as alumni believe they should continue to have a prominent voice in the critical affairs of the university.

These two environments—the internal and external—have somewhat fluid borders, as recruiters are often former graduates; donors are alumni and employers; and the members of the board of directors hold multiple positions as pillars of this fairly conservative city. This all requires a unique balancing act for the most astute leader.

Meet the CEO

John had the right background for such a difficult job: credentials, experience, and personality. At his former university, another complex state system, he had held a top administative post and proven his capability for managing large numbers of faculty and students. In person, he was affable and possessed a demonstrable knowledge of the considerable inner workings of university life.

John began his tenure on solid footing, poised to move from the honeymoon period to maneuvering the school toward fiscal solvency, while simultaneously advancing its reputation. He had no shortage of good ideas, vision, and charisma. The timing too was excellent: The new president took the reigns at the university following a rash of negative public press about the former president, who was seen as having a rather extravagant manner. The welcome contrast and excitement of the entire community at the time of the change fostered a climate that made John stand out as stellar in comparison to his unpopular predecessor. Thus, the new president was welcomed initially with high expectations for leading a more tempered personal life and returning the university to fiscal stability and high respectability.

Aside from the initial faux pas of holding an extravagant welcoming party, as well as an expensive remodeling of the president's house, which led to an unfavorable comparison to his spendthrift predecessor, his term began in a honeymoon fashion. In the first two years, John worked at building positive relationships with students and faculty with regard to curriculum advancements and also generated concern for much needed attention to diversity. Both groups couldn't say enough great things about this man as someone who was "finally listening to student and faculty concerns."

Affability aside, as time went on, the administration began to perceive him as ill prepared at meetings, not fully versed in complex issues, and one to take on issues passionately while neglecting other, equally pressing concerns that remained on the table. In the midst of the post-honeymoon (or "reality hits hard" period) while moving the university toward a more balanced budget, a somewhat unusual issue surfaced. A contingency of students, faculty, and staff were lobbying for health-care benefits for partners when the partner happened to be the same sex. John saw this as a reasonable request whose time had come. He unilaterally supported the request, which would provide the benefits to same-sex partners, sidestepping arguments from other constituents whom he regarded as fuddy duddies.

Case Analysis

What John failed to appreciate was that the issue was not really about benefits—it was perceived as sanctioning behavior that many in the community and on the board of directors viewed as deviant and running counter to the mores of the community. "So what," he thought. "This town is too conservative anyway."

But perhaps even more important, this decision would hit the largest health-care provider of the university hard, as it meant the health-care-provider contract would change. The head of this health-care provider sat on the board of trustees.

John behaved in a unilateral fashion, believing in the merit of an idea. By taking a stand in favor of one large group of actors (and in our terms, a group of his dependencies), he simultaneously violated another group of critical decision makers. Unfortunately for John, this was the group with power.

John made some students happy, and he made some faculty and staff happy. In his prior role as dean, keeping these groups happy would have been the key to success. But organizations are not just about internal environments; they are not just about dependencies we can readily see. This is a common challenge to managers who move up the corporate ladder—at one level, attending to internal constituencies fosters their success. As they move up, the base of constituents widens, broadens, and is sometimes out of immediate sight. Lateral relationships, if you will, become a mixture of internal and external groups, with a complex interplay between the two environs.

In this case, some of the really critical constituents or dependencies were literally outside of John's vision. But not for long. Those he had violated internally, some top-level faculty and administrators, moved rather quickly to form a coalition with the board of trustees. Even though John was boss, the relationships between the long-term faculty and administrators had been strong for many years prior to John's arrival.

In rather short order, John was perceived as working in ways antithetical to key internal and external interests. He was Mr. Outsider. In turn, John reacted against this coalition of people who were no longer his allies. He began to avoid meetings with what he came to view as unyielding and retroactive administrators, became short tempered with some faculty whose loyalty seemed dubious, and refused to see other groups altogether. This avoidance, withdrawal, and in some cases, aggressive behavior caused him to quickly be labeled as difficult, unapproachable, and a multitude of other, less flattering adjectives. The stream of behavior led to further difficulties between John, the tenured faculty, and the board of directors. In rather short order, there was a new headline on the front page of the city newspaper, proclaiming, "(John): Out." These two words pretty well summed up the political situation, from accolades of welcome to being out of power with accompanying blame in just a few short years.

We present a summary of John's difficulties with full acknowledgment that this situation is hardly unique. Almost every week we seem to read about other giants, smart men and women who rise to power on the basis of intelligence, charm, wit, hard work, and genuine talent, only to be "done in" by corporate politics or their own lack of ability to manage those politics. At present, the same-sex issue is also in the news. Large-scale demonstrations by students with major support by community groups, the ACLU, and others are trying to force and embarrass the university into providing these benefits among other provisions. The university is taking a hard line—and is being sued.

What causes able leaders such as John to make mistakes that are so easy for us to see in "Monday-morning quarterback" style? In the following section, we highlight some of the myths and mistakes about power that played out in this case, followed by a resource and dependency analysis. This analysis demonstrates the importance of understanding not just one or two groups that may be impacted by our ideas and programs, as in the earlier cases. This case analysis also demonstrates the complex, interdependent nature of these groups. In short, dependencies don't exist in isolation in organization—the context is critical to fully comprehend the less visible groups and the interconnectedness of dependencies. We also highlight the role of the external environment, the influence of which was misunderstood by John. Finally, in doing the ABCs of political relationships, we demonstrate the challenge of affecting change in this type of politically charged environment and also how executives should think about change.

Understanding What John Did Wrong: Myths about Power

First, we consider the mistakes John made because they are germane to many situations where people rise to power. Two myths about power and mistakes about lateral relationships are dominant here. The first myth is again the pervasive myth that power and authority are synonymous. John, like many newly appointed CEOs, came to a dangerous recognition too late.

The second myth demonstrated here is also pervasive: that power, rather than dependency on lateral relationships, is the key to success. We have said that power is more about dependency than authority. We also hold that the higher one is propelled in the hierarchy of power, the harder it seems to keep sight of the reality of dependence. To make it all the more complicated, dependencies change and they are sometimes not particularly visible.

Here are some lessons for John and other top-level managers:

Lesson 1: Know thy dependencies—not just the visible ones, but the unseen dependencies.

Lesson 2: Learn thy dependencies wants and needs.

Lesson 3: Study the interconnectedness of thy dependencies.

Lesson 4: Avoid unilateral behavior in complex organizations—that is, think through the effects and consequences of actions.

The Resources

What are the critical resources of a university? If we were to take away all the embellishments, the faculty, students, and finances are the critical resources. Although top-notch faculty will always be sought after and presumably valued, in today's environment, there are unemployed Ph.D.s. Although some would disagree with us (and others would prefer we keep quiet about this), faculty clout is at a lower ebb than it has been in past eras.

The real competition in universities is for students and dollars. And so we ask, Who controls those resources? One critical index for attracting students is the job-placement rate; another is the reputation held by employers and alumni. The local media also influences reputation. In a midsized city, the media has much to gain from the stories of universities, as they have a reciprocal relationship: The media is given lots of fodder for news stories from research, student news, and sports, and the university's reputation is enhanced by the media coverage. University budgets at state schools have much to do with decisions by state government. As in all political scenarios, it is important to examine the general resources of the industry to get at the context in which one is managing.

And so we ask, What are the critical resources and thus dependencies of this context? In sum, they are the students, local business community, alumni, media, and state government. From here, the reputation will be made or broken, and financial solvency will be dependent upon that.

Internally, the dependencies include the students, the faculty (largely the senior faculty), and the board of directors. Thus, John's ability to hold on to power would have much to do with keeping favor with these groups as a priority in his actions. Engaging in actions that favored one of these priorities at the expense of another would be a prediction for failure.

The ABCs of the Political Organization

The ABC diagram is complex and highlights essential resource and dependencies (see Figure 11.1). John would be essentially in the middle of a circle of dependencies. Here, we limit it to the desired outcome of attempting to change one university policy, which many pundits called his fatal mistake. We disagree and support the merit of his idea; but the way John went about it was naive.

The ABC Analysis

The ABC diagram highlights the nature of the external control and the larger environmental context. It also illustrates the numerous targets the CEO needs to think about, only a few of which he actually holds real authority over. In some ways, the CEO has even more de-

Figure 11.1
The University President and the Faculty

X = A wants a change in policy.
X' = A wants to keep students happy.
X' = A wants to advance his reputation.
X' = A wants to do the "right" thing.

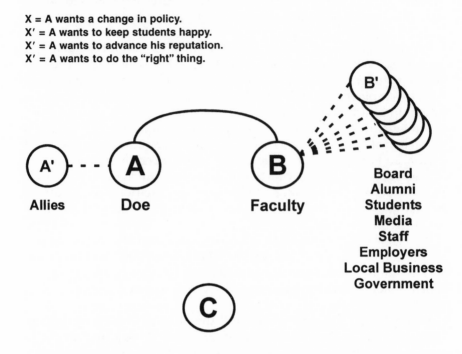

Organization Context = The culture is fairly conservative. There is a fluid boundary between internal and external environments. There are interconnected dependencies. Fifty percent of the alumni are local, and there is strong external control.

pendencies than individuals at lower levels of management—a difficult concept, fostering an even more challenging work environment.

Actions Available to the Agent

To begin, an action plan would need to be mindful of the external nature of control. In Chapter 2, we discussed the external control of organizations and how critical it is for managers to remain mindful of the dynamic nature of it. John had lost sight of the external controls governing this university. In this university, much of the power was in the financial resources and in those who controlled local business, the government, and in some measure, the overall success of the local economy who supported this school profoundly. Thus, the reputation which determined the fate of the university and its external control was pivotal. The business interests of the board were nontrivial. John's actions threatened those.

Counting the Costs

Along with considering the interests of the external environment, it is critical for the agent (even CEOs) to count the costs before embarking on political action. In this situation, the gain was relatively small compared to the personal cost of alienation to John. One could argue that John stood by his principles and should be applauded. We don't dispute the nobility of such a stand. Unfortunately, in taking the position as "Lone Ranger" against these types of costs, the agent and the plan are likely to be very short lived, as happened here. The plan was killed; the agent who pushed it was very soon off to distant pastures.

What to Do When the Cost Is Too High
(But the Conviction Is Also)

That people, even at the top, routinely fail in implementing their ideas raises the question of whether plans that are highly controversial and essentially disrupt the status quo should be scrapped? That route would most certainly have been the safer political route here. Nevertheless, we are not so old as to suggest hiding from controversial plans once one is wise enough to appreciate the cost of controversy. That route is too easy and against the spirit of this book.

John's plan would have required a great amount of planning and rigorous analysis, along with commitment from the numerous targets affected by it. It would need to be done in concert with and not counter to some of the critical interests of his board and local business. In short, we suggest that with extraordinary ideas, extraordinary rigor needs to be devoted to the planning and implementation process. The following steps are crucial:

- Do the dependency and resource analysis.
- Consider the context.
- Analyze the external controls that may be hidden.
- Count the costs to all constituents—beginning with the agent.
- Consider the X—what is really wanted here. Is it defined in a way that is most favorable to the many interests?
- Consider the A primes. Others with whom to build a coalition (even at the top, coalition is important).
- Expand beyond immediate targets to the numerous alternate targets who must carry out the change.

• Consider the enormity of this policy change and plan it as a process over a time period sufficient to build incremental support.

The principle lesson we wish to evoke here is the notion that planning political action or thinking through consequences of relatively mild changes or "good ideas" is very often foreign to people at the top, as was John in this scenario. The tendency to equate authority with power and to ignore context, costs, external control, and dependencies is great and sometimes absolutely fatal.

What should new leaders do to avoid such scenarios? We attempt to answer this very question in the following case, which offers a comparative view. It is about another CEO who also managed a complex, political environment. This individual brought large-scale, productive changes to the university and ten years later is continuing to reap personal and professional accolades, the most important of all being an extraordinarily successful university. An accreditation board recently lauded the school as a model for other universities to follow.

A SUCCESSFUL CASE OF CULTURAL CHANGE

This president (whom we will call Henry) took his new position in the late 1980s as president of a university in crisis. Suffering from financial woes, a demoralized faculty, an inattentive board, and a culture which preferred the glory days of the past to the challenges of the present, he wondered if this new position was prestigious or precarious.

What some new CEOs do in such a "near-the-brink" scenario is to engage in turnaround actions—and quickly. They mobilize a new idea or agenda to revitalize the troops and rally folks around a motivational direction, even if the plan or agenda is not well thought out. Sometimes this comes in the form of a new product. For example, there were four new CEOs in five years at Apple, each taking the reigns with a spirited agenda for success and often championing a new product. For the most part, and as evidenced by their short reign, they achieved little long-term success, despite great effort. Too, the management fads of the past twenty years advocate large-scale change, restructuring, and reengineering to turn firms around.

Sometimes, taking over damaged organizations means giving immediate attention to the bottom line by engaging in such actions as mergers, selling off nonprofitable divisions, or, more painfully, letting human resources go in vast numbers. We needn't look very far in American business to see these short-term fixes. The daily newspapers and nightly news remind us of the dynamic pace of business operations. We barely react at news of twenty thousand people or more being "downsized" in one quick chop (even though downsizing creates other problems for organizations, such as maintaining quality research and development, and is predictably detrimental to morale). Yet, people with flashy agendas, which often include such short-term fixes, are the very folks who often get promoted—everyone loves a plan or solid direction in times of uncertainty.

We could discourse on the detrimental effects of short-term fixes, but suffice to say that new executives are often the first to attempt the quick fix when faced with difficult scenarios. But our focus here is to illustrate a different approach. What did Henry do when taking the reigns of a troubled organization, and what does it tell us about the management of lateral relationships?

Unlike a lot of CEOs who take the top posts and treat their newfound positions as "authority central," this one viewed his role as being in the center of the organization. From the onset of his presidency, he used the phrase "my colleagues," which denoted more than a salutation— it also denoted a way of "seeing" his role as *part* of the organization, not above it.

In the early chapters of this book, we have illustrated at length the notion of dependencies, resources, and the external control of firms. And, in the preceding cases, we have demonstrated how many new CEOs and middle-level managers were rendered insolvent by neglecting to consider and carefully analyze their dependencies for action. This theme of neglecting core dependencies runs through management at the middle, at the almost top, and even at the very top, and it is the most essential component of effectiveness at any level.

To look at this CEO, we begin by addressing his understanding and management of key resources and dependencies. As we described in the preceding case, the key resources of this industry are students, faculty, finances, and the reputation that holds the key resources together. Without reputation, the students, faculty, and finances are not going to survive in today's competitive university environment. We could picture this new president at the center of these resources in order to highlight who and what comprise the key dependencies of the university (see Figure 11.2).

The ABC Analysis

This view presents a different model than the typical organizational chart that places a president in the top box. This, model, we believe, is a better representation of the realities of managing than the "org chart," which depicts a commander in chief at the top with subordinates beneath, or, if we may borrow from an older structure of management, an administrative or military model.

At the same time, this model doesn't imply any less leadership or even authority. Some of our students initially question this: "But the guy is still in charge, isn't he?" Sure, he (and even she, in rare cases) is

Figure 11.2
A Private University Setting

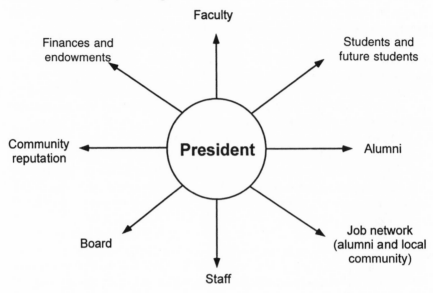

in charge and could probably fire or control the people in the groups represented around the circle. But, for getting things done, this view of authority within the context of lateral relationships reflects a clearer picture because it begs the critical question, Whose support is needed for effective change? At the same time, it provides a more lucid view of the dependencies that can thwart change or the implementation of good and even great ideas, as we witnessed in the earlier cases of Lisa, the hospital COO, and Jim, the consulting manager.

In sum, by seeing himself at the center of the circle, Henry could well say "my colleagues" and think about change from the inside out through all these groups.

President Henry's Good Idea

As in all the cases of this book, Henry had a "good idea" for improving his organization. He wanted to change it from a sinking university that had had its heyday into a premier, top-ranked university. Here is, in a nutshell, what he did.

First, he focused on the two top priorities, which represented in our terms his critical resources and dependencies. He focused on the people who comprised the organization, communicating a direction of change consistently. He worked with the faculty on boosting morale by finding money to improve salaries. He hired a new internal manager who shared his vision. The vice president, or provost in university lingo, focused on building and improving one of the more critical resources of a university—its faculty.

Both began to communicate an identity of change and progress, of building from the inside out, of rewarding the behaviors they wanted to see, such as real quality in all aspects of behavior, particularly student treatment.

The model of promotion, as well as who and what were promoted, began to change. Universities, like many businesses, are famous for saying they "want" certain behaviors and pontificate about those "values" in speeches, but then the higher-ups continue to reward old behaviors. What do they get? The old behaviors, of course, coupled with frustrated employees. Here, the reward system changed to be consistent with, not antithetical to, the desired behaviors and direction of moving upward via the quality of the people.

Henry also worked with what was possibly the second strongest university asset or resource—a very strong, loyal, and local alumni base, many of whom were graduates of its once (and now, once again) prestigious law school and business schools. A hundred years of graduates, the majority of whom had settled and in many cases were quite prominent in the local business environment, represented a rich and vital resource. This resource had been nodded to but not utilized prior to Henry's tenure. The president fostered the obvious connections with this critical resource and became stellar at raising money, which in turn enabled him to build and expand the universities physical structure, recruit increasingly top-notch students, all the while maintaining a scholarship base and faculty with established reputations.

The alumni connection represents a good example of the external control of organizations. This resource is neither internal nor external, but presents one of the most critical links between the organization's internal and external worlds. Alumni are pivotal toward managing a university's most vital resource—its reputation. At the same time, the alumni resource was understood for what it is—a source of funding, involvement, and recruitment, as well as consisting of those who put forward the university's reputation in the larger community (as they have strong motivation to do so).

While quadrupling enrollments, building reputation, and expanding the infrastructure, Henry worked predominately on nurturing the internal culture and retained a focus on the core dependency of the university—the people.

In sum, this social construction of relationships first fostered a culture of excellence. People want to do well in this setting and are drawn to it. People referred to it as the school on the "up and up." It was also consistently high ranked. We offer that this was because the units rose to excellence in concert, internally building the culture while promoting the value of treating individuals well. In comparison to the case of failure, we believe this president managed both the internal and external critical dependencies well.

CONCLUSION

CEOs face failure—routinely. All the talent, capability, hard work, and hutzpah it takes to get to the top is no guarantee of staying or of effectiveness. We have argued that managing at the top, as well as at the bottom and the middle, is about the effective diagnosis of lateral networks, relationships, resources, and dependencies. It is about knowing how to direct and work within these complex power and political networks.

In this comparitive rendering of the cases of two university CEOs, we see two talented individuals who have risen to the top of their fields, both as individuals and finally as administers over the course of twenty to thirty years of dedicated effort. It is safe to assume they are competent and smart. They are also well versed in the nuances of "people skills" as well as the hard-core skills of managing difficult financial, regulatory, and external political and economic challenges and constraints.

Yet, one failed and one succeeded, largely as a product of being skilled at conducting the complex inner networks of politics and the web of lateral relationships that spans both internal and external environments. From their example, we offer that effective management of lateral relationships is never merely about the tasks of the industry, or the goals, aspirations, or myriad good ideas, directions, services, or products. It is always about a template that takes into account the laterally constructed relationships. It involves

- Analyzing resources.
- Diagnosing dependencies.
- Assessing the external control of the organization.
- Taking into account dynamic contexts.
- Effective and rigorous strategy for seeing and managing the dependency relationships.

This is a simple template. We have worked to keep it simple, as a path toward effective action and as being applicable to a wide variety of settings. This model works for the middle-level manager, for the manager without authority, and for the manager with all the authority and none of the power.

12

Conclusion

Our driving goal in this book has been to demonstrate the link between theory and practical application for effective management in the new lateral organization. Our sole purpose has been to show that plans, objectives, and great ideas can be successful, and to provide specific tools for achieving that success. People *can* and *should* be successful in their organizational life, but *only* through fully comprehending and working within the social context of power and politics.

In the twenty-first century, the ability to work within lateral organizations becomes all the more vital and we believe this ability will increasingly separate the successful from the frustrated.

MYTHS ABOUT THE LATERAL ORGANIZATION

To be sure, there are several myths about the new lateral organization. We summarize here a few of the myths of lateral organizations and our tools for successfully managing them.

The first is that lateral organizations are not easy to manage. We've written about organizations that have and are likely to have more lateral structures and less hierarchy and less formal rules. We emphasize that the difference in structure does not imply a soft or, as some call it, a "touchy–feely" atmosphere. Less hierarchy implies more politics, not less. And as some rules in the new organization are less formally and clearly defined, power and political relationships often become all the more intense.

Consider the example of an organization whose new CEO advocated less hierarchy and preached more empowerment to employees.

This CEO decided the new form of "his" organization should involve no departments, so that people (and their ideas) would be less compartmentalized. In the process, he hoped to diminish some of the political undercurrents that had been divisive among the various divisions. The theory sounded good—less formal divisions, more cross-fertilization of ideas. Unfortunately, the culture of this organization and the mind-set of its people were not quite up to this structural change. People stayed in, or created new fiefdoms. People from one side of the building didn't do lunch with the other side. Competition over resources remained and even intensified, as individuals engaged in power jockeying to determine who would achieve higher status in the "departmentless organization." Instead of working through department heads, people "learned" that individual lobbying of the CEO was the way to "be heard." They learned too that their colleagues ended up with more (in terms of power and resources) than they had themselves, due in large part to the varied skills of winning favor with the CEO. All of this served to reinforce the model of lobbying privately for pet projects, agendas, or resource needs in hiring. Overtime, the CEO became overwhelmed. The span of control of a hundred employees and no division heads to serve as buffers for filtering requests or allocating resources overwhelmed him and diverted his attention from external matters.

It was difficult for employees to sort out who really held the power in this departmentless structure. The organization became even more politically oriented and the power dynamics more intense. The winners, those with an "in" with the CEO, gained in some cases to the detriment of the larger good of the business. The losers remained perplexed. This example of an organization that eliminated divisions, breezily seeking to eliminate political divisiveness, may paint an unduly bleak picture. Nevertheless, it highlights three critical points: (1) Politics is a pervasive part of organizations; (2) structure changes can't eliminate politics; and (3) creating lateral organizations does not create organizations that are any easier to manage.

Like all the cases in this book, the organization discussed is quite real. It has a reputation for being an arduous and highly political place to work. Individuals blame other individuals, while the business has gone through two more CEOs in the past five years. In short, lateral isn't equivalent to easy or soft, but has many aspects that are quite hard and all the more arduous. New rules doesn't mean no rules. And, as we have asserted throughout, less hierarchy and formal authority can complicate, rather than simplify, the internal workings of firms.

The second set of myths we want to expose is that there are no quick fixes for managing lateral organizations. As this book goes to press, one of the authors is researching a book on faddism—the origins of

American and international management fads that promise quick and utopian solutions. While the philosophy and form of fads differ, common to all fads is the promise of a better, idealized organizational environment. Equally common is that most fads and quick-fix solutions fail. Likewise, we do not mean to imply that all organizational problems are solvable through the understandings provided here. As is discussed in Chapter 3, dependencies are constructed. Sometimes deciding the cost is not quite worth it, nor is it the most effective thing to do. When situations of working for unyielding bosses or being caught in power plays that have more to do with underlying external control and resource allocation, analyzing the situational realities intelligently and with adequate tools to do so may save years of fruitless frustration. Sometimes, there is nothing to do to change an organization, as hard as that is to admit. We like to think we can change our environments. Surely, we think that with above-average intelligence, armed with degrees, know-how, hutzpah, and political savvy, we must be capable of rendering appropriate change. Clear analysis helps to separate the situations we can affect, from those we just may be powerless to change. And, knowing the personal cost in attempting to be effective is also a critical portion of the equation. Sometimes, the personal cost is not worth it; sometimes it is, either for professional or moral reasons. We advocate knowing the difference and making a conscious choice.

At the same time, this book was motivated by seeing a generation of M.B.A. students and clients who *have* found success and effectiveness. We can write confidently about these tools because they work. We have taught these theories to several thousand M.B.A. students and modeled thousands of problems using the tools presented here. Many have had the good fortune of applying these skills to their organizational dilemmas and they report the stories of their success through new ways of understanding old conflicts and a greater sense of power and control over their own organizational lives. We think it's good they did, because trends suggest that learning to manage within lateral organizations is all the more important for success.

TRENDS FOR THE NEW MILLENNIUM: LATERAL ORGANIZATIONS

Trends in business suggest that lateral rather than hierarchically structured organizations will continue to become more common. Managers will need to consider implications of the following trends. Most particularly, organizations are poised to face ongoing transition. For example, downsizing, and the replacement and reorganization of workers at all levels, which has become commonplace during the 1990s, is likely to continue, with new waves of mergers, acquisitions, and the global reorganization of plants and industries. As geographic locations shift, authority shifts; workers face ongoing reorganizations. In short, the old order of business, rules, power, and loyalties will continue to change. This means an ongoing challenge for workers and managers in overseeing relationships.

Within these reorganizations, technological progress will persist to change the way work is done and, for our purposes, the way relationships are managed. Technological progress in electronic communication, for example, solves some problems, but also advances lateral networks. As e-mail replaces memos, it is no longer necessary to send memos through hierarchical structures. In many organizations, authority may be weakened as communication advances and networks between and among employees intensifies. In short, our technological advances mean your skills in interpersonal and lateral relationships will be all the more vital.

Technology, too, fosters the ongoing reduction in hierarchical levels and a replacement with team based structures. Self-managed teams, such as we witness en masse in companies like Motorola and Saturn, mean managers and workers alike must learn the skills inherent in lateral contexts. Teams are expected to be productive, to manage internal conflicts smoothly, and to make progress without the benefit of layers of authority and command.

Another trend that intensifies the need for lateral-relationship management is more diversity at the work place. The increasingly international and gender-diverse work force also brings with it a less homogenous work force. While a good thing in our view, this also means that managers will need to acquire new skills in lateral relationship management, as communication and behavior differences are negotiated.

Other demographic changes threaten to foster polarity at the work place. In specific, as the work force continues to age, and the retirement age increases, there will be more workers over sixty. There will be continued competition for managerial positions. Ongoing changes, along with demographic trends, suggest an elimination of certain career ladders. All of this implies a predictable increase in competition for position, advancement, and power.

These organizational trends are hardly stellar or prophetic. However, we highlight them here because these ongoing changes imply that new dexterity will be required for workers in general and managers in particular to cope, to survive, and to achieve in the ever-changing work place.

The dexterity we have promoted and outlined involves the application of the theories of power and politics and the skills of lateral managing relationships and networks. The simple fact is that most businesses are not currently run by those trained in lateral-relationship-focused management. Rather, the majority of top- and middle-level managers running today's organizations have learned and experienced a management style more appropriate to yesterday's organizations of hierarchical structures, rules, homogeneity, loyalty, and stability. These older managers have been weaned on organizations with far different cultures, different paradigms of management, such as the scientific-management paradigm with an efficiency, or one-way-of-doing-things, focus, administrative models, division of labor, hierarchy, rules, and procedures. The majority of today's managers are not particularly well equipped to work within the new climate. This underlies some of the tension of today's organizations, which is unlikely to abate anytime soon. And, as we shift toward team-based and networked structures, implied psychological contracts, negotiated environments, and new interplay with community and environments, this confluence of ingredients suggests that the work place is likely to become more rather than less arduous, intense, and for many, puzzling. Neither yesterday's problem-solving models or today's creative tools of influence and self-help techniques are likely to prove adequate.

At the same time, the tension between the new form of organization and the old school of managers is that many of the popular management philosophies aren't keeping pace with, or even sometimes hide, work place realities. We are referring to the management philosophies flaunted as quick-fix solutions and those that herald a more idealistic work place. For example, the new form of the work place incited and brought into vogue a management philosophy of worker participation and employee empowerment over the past ten years. Management's version of employee empowerment often meant ask the right questions, or, sure, make a suggestion, but make sure it is a politically correct one and doesn't embarrass your boss. Be sure to stay within the chain of political command, even if we no longer have the formal division and hierarchy. In other words, the theory is new, but the reality is not. This often created a puzzling environment for workers.

Some large-scale efforts, themselves sound in theory, are increasingly difficult to sustain in today's business world. For example, consider one such transformational effort of TQM involving participatory management, employee empowerment, quality product and process focus, and group decision making, which was brought to vogue in the later 1980s and 1990s. Some of the companies that were proponents of these promotions, such as Xerox, are now finding the need to pull back from the philosophy, as downsizing and needs to cut cost for competitive survival override the very best intentions. Many models of management, which should have made a huge difference in managing in the new lateral organizations, are simply difficult to sustain in a business world increasingly pushed toward international competitiveness.

Participatory management, team-based approaches, and concepts such as empowerment and total quality are costly in time and people and are sometimes inadequate in the face of a competitive business world. The philosophies are often not sustained or sustainable. That is the simple, harsh reality.

So, where does this leave the average worker, manager, and ambitious new hire? For one, it leaves us with organizations that are more complex than any of our current managerial paradigms afford us. In short, most buzz words are simply that, and managerial philosophies fall short of the nitty-gritty realities.

And so, we began this book asserting that organizations are complex. There are no quick fixes here. Neither self-help style management approaches or utopian models are adequate in today's lateral organization. Each situation requires specific diagnosis, rigorous planning, careful strategic analysis, mapping, and a game plan as difficult as any type of problem you will ever want to solve.

Yet, we have also maintained that it is well worth this level of analysis and rigor, because careers are often determined by successful problem-solving strategies. As we demonstrated in the cases of Lisa, the hospital chief operating officer, and the university presidents, getting to the top is only half the battle. Power and position can be quite fleeting. Retaining power via managerial responsibilities or position revolves around successful political management of lateral relationships. And, for those who haven't yet arrived at such lofty levels of upper management, solving lateral organizational dilemmas is a required prerequisite toward horizontal advancement.

We can think of no other arena in life, aside from one's own family, where it matters more to be successful. In today's world, we spend much of our lifetime at that place called "work." For many professionals, the balance of home and work even becomes tilted toward prioritizing work. We choose where to live, with all of its implications for our families and our other pursuits, based on "where we work." We define ourselves largely by what we "do." Think about the last time someone asked you what do you do. Answering that you build bird houses, coach Little League, read to your kids, or carpool, although you may do those things in large quantities, is not the expected answer. Your job title is what defines who you are to a stranger. Learning to manage our work lives, even if we are not formally called managers, is simply one of the very most critical skills we can ever learn and practice. And that is why we have written this book.

We believe the skills for negotiating the political environments of work can and should be learned with as much attention, rigor, and care as any other undertaking. Yet, it is not uncommon for people to spend more time planning a summer vacation or their weddings than they give to planning strategies to achieve their organizational goals. That is why our model involves far more time than any of the self-help or quick-fix solutions we have seen promoted. As we reflect upon the work stories of the people profiled in this book, we see how many experienced failure, despite an abundance of talent and hard work. As they came to understand their failures, they were able to apply themselves again toward successful careers. Neither blaming their "abusive bosses" any longer nor their own stupidity, they came to understand the organizational realities that had confounded them.

A strategy for the successful implementation of a good idea takes place in one-by-one, plan-by-plan, and step-by-step fashion. No utopian businesses, no utopian organizational theories to right all the wrongs, and no amount of self-help, social influence, charm, or perseverance can substitute for it.

Bibliography

Cohen, Allen R., & Bradford, David L. (1989). *Influence without authority*. New York: John Wiley & Sons.

Cotton, Chester C. (1976). The measurement of power-balancing styles. *Administrative Science Quarterly, 21*, 307–319.

Emerson, Richard M. (1962). Power–dependence relations. *American Sociological Review, 27*, 33–41.

Kanter, Rosabeth M. (1977). *Men and women of the corporation*. New York: Basic Books.

Kipnis, David. (1980). *The powerbuilders*. Chicago: University of Chicago Press.

Kipnis, David; Schmidt, Stuart; & Wilkenson, Ian. (1980). Interorganizational influence tactics: Explorations in getting one's way. *Journal of Applied Psychology, 65*, 440–457.

Kotter, John P. (1995). *The new rules*. Boston: Harvard Business School Press.

Pfeffer, Jeffrey. (1981). *Power in organizations*. Marshfield, MA: Pitman.

Pfeffer, Jeffrey. (1992). *Managing with power*. Boston: Harvard Business School Press.

Salancik, Gerald R., & Pfeffer, Jeffrey. (1977, Winter). Who gets power and how they hold onto it: A strategic-contingency model of power. *Organizational Dynamics*, 3–21.

Salancik, Gerald R., & Pfeffer, Jeffrey. (1978). *The external control of organizations: A resource dependence perspective*. New York: Harper & Row.

Index

Context, 135, 137; definition, 39, 135, 137; dependencies, 117; examining, 101, 139, 159; the idea in, 109; manipulation of, 106–107, 141; neglected, 124; resources, 117; social, 6–7, 10, 46–47
Corporate-level task forces, 132
Corporate politics, 161
Corporate support group, 147
Cost-benefit analysis, 114
Costs, counting, 165
Costs, nonmonetary, 83–84; to key actors, 133; to other relationships, 85; of precedent, 86; of reputation, 86–88
Critical resources, 162–163
Cultural–anthropological analysis, 30–31

Dependencies, 40, 101, 131, 143; changes in, 155; perceived, 35
Dependent relationship, 38, 63, 66; anatomy of, 44, 79
Desire (or X), modified, 107
Desires, as social constructs, 73
Diagnostic tools, 4
Downsizing, 166

Economic-analysis consulting firm, 24–26
Emerson, Richard M., 33, 42, 55
Exemption from rules, 59
External control, 17–18; analysis, 33; factors, 50, 137

Fairness, perception of, 14
Fayol, Henry, 137

Goals: alternative, 51–52; defined, 82

Hewlett Packard, 26–27
Hierarchy and politics, 171, 172

Idea failure, despite support, 93
Ideas, reasons for failure, 5
Implementation planning, 113, 114, 117
Interests considered, 108

Internal constituencies, 161
Internal environments, 161
Interpersonal power relationships, 3
Interpersonal skills, 39
Intractable contexts, 149
Investment, as a cost, 88

Labor division, 10
Lateral organization trends: demographic change, 174; diversity, 174; employee empowerment, 175; less hierarchy, 173; self-help techniques, 175; technology, 174
Lateral relationships: diagrammed, 50–52; myths, 171–173; political realities, 4, 8, 9
LIR (Labor and Industrial Relations) School, 33, 40, 42, 44, 50
Losing project, being assigned, 150–152

Management fads, 172–173
Management paradigm, 4
Manipulation, 66
Means versus ends, 88
Mentor, 154
Middle-level managers, 135
Motivation, 112

"Near-the-brink" scenario, 166
Norms, social, 46–47

Occupational Safety and Health Administration (OSHA), 107, 129–130, 131, 143
One-down. *See* Power imbalance, context of
Organization, defined, 17
Organizational goals versus realities, 113
Organizational paradigm, 29
Organization wide theories, 2
Org chart, 167

Paradigms, historical nature of, 29
Paying the tax, 105, 139
Personality conflict, 95
Pfeffer, Jeffrey, 17

ABOUT THE AUTHORS

Margaret Brindle is Associate Professor at George Mason University. Formerly, she taught M.B.A. and Executive Education at Carnegie Mellon University for ten years. She is also a former manager and R.N. and Professor in the School of Business at Duquesne University, where she taught strategy and organizational behavior. She has been published in a number of journals and serves on several editorial boards.

Lisa A. Mainiero is Professor of Management in the School of Business at Fairfield University. She has been published in numerous journals and is the author of *Office Romance* (1989) and co-author of *Developing Managerial Skills* (1989). Dr. Mainiero also served on the Editorial Board of the Academy of Management Executives and chaired the Women in Management (now Gender and Diversity in Organizations) Division of the Academy of Management.

ISBN 1-56720-334-5

EAN

9 781567 203349

90000>

HARDCOVER BAR CODE